THE Fretboard Journal

NUMBER 22. SUMMER 2011.

www.fretboardjournal.com
FACEBOOK www.facebook.com/fretboardjournal
TWITTER www.twitter.com/fbjournal
www.twitter.com/selmerguy

PUBLISHER Jason Verlinde
EDITOR-AT-LARGE Michael John Simmons
OFFICE MANAGER Ryan Richter
PROOFREADER Kim Runciman

DESIGN & PRODUCTION David Ruszczynski
PHOTO PRE-PRESS Justin Myers

CONTRIBUTING WRITERS

Mark Demaray, Rich Kienzle, Doc Simpson, John Thomas,
Andy Volk, Tom Walzem, Joe Yanuziello

CONTRIBUTING PHOTOGRAPHERS

Rachel Bleckman, Peter DiAntoni, Lynn Donaldson,
John Peden, Thomas Petillo, Doug Van Doren

NEWSSTAND CONSULTANT Ellen Sugarman

THE FRETBOARD JOURNAL

2221 NW 56th St., Suite 101
Seattle, WA 98107
(206) 706-3252

NUMBER 22, SUMMER 2011. *The Fretboard Journal* (ISSN 1558-
0326) is published quarterly by Occasional Publishing, Inc., 2221 NW
56th St., Suite 101, Seattle, WA 98107. Periodicals postage paid at Seattle,
WA and additional mailing offices. All rights reserved. Reproduction
without permission is prohibited. POSTMASTER: Please send address
changes to The Fretboard Journal, 2221 NW 56th St., Suite 101, Seattle,
WA 98107.

U.S. SUBSCRIPTIONS $40.00 for four issues (one year); $75.00
for eight issues (two years). Available at www.fretboardjournal.com or
(877) 373-8273.
FOREIGN SUBSCRIPTIONS Visit www.fretboardjournal.com.
MOVING? Please email (subscriptions@fretboardjournal.com) or call
us with your new address. The post office will not automatically forward
your subscription.
ADVERTISING Contact Jason Verlinde at
jason@fretboardjournal.com.
COPYRIGHT © 2011 by Occasional Publishing, Inc.
All rights reserved. Printed in China.

COVER: Jackson Browne with one of
his coveted Gibson Roy Smeck guitars.
PHOTO: PETER DIANTONI

RIGHT: The first electric guitar that Jeff Traugott made for
Charlie Hunter visits Traugott's shop for a quick adjustment before
heading back on the road. The seven-string neck combines four
strings from a standard guitar and three strings from a bass.
(See the story on page 48 for an explanation of how this works.)

THE Fretboard Journal

NUMBER 22. SUMMER 2011.

DEPARTMENTS

4 **Opening Notes**

126 **Contributors**

128 **Tailpiece**

COVER STORY: JACKSON BROWNE

84 **Load Out**
On the road with Jackson Browne
and dozens of vintage Gibsons
By John Thomas

96 **Stay**
Jackson Browne, in his own words,
on songwriting
Introduction by Jason Verlinde

108 **A Roy Smeck Primer**
Modifying vintage guitars is usually
discouraged, but not here

FEATURES

6 **The Guitarists' Bucket List**
99 things we think you should do,
at some point
By the Fretboard Journal

22 **Mother of Pearl**
Kathy and Jimmi Wingert make
guitars a family business
By Michael John Simmons

30 **Dynasty**
Jazz great John Pizzarelli upholds
the family tradition
By Rich Kienzle

48 **Engine Check**
Guitarist Charlie Hunter and luthier
Jeff Traugott go under the hood of
their ongoing collaborations
Introduction by Michael John Simmons

58 **Classically Trained**
Muriel Anderson walks the fine line
between bluegrass, fingerstyle and
flamenco music
By Andy Volk

68 **Easy Being Green**
The recycling artistry of motocross-
racing, wood-logging, knife-
building, fly-fishing luthier
Larry Pogreba
By Doc Simpson

CASE STUDIES

12 Triple Play
Three consecutive serial numbered
1937 Tonk Bros. Washburns

16 The Other Loar
A 1924 Gibson tenor lute

20 Jailhouse Hula
William Stedman's Hawaiian guitar

110 All in the Family
Luthier John Arnold pays homage
to an old Martin

115 Case Closed
A 1920s ukulele case with a story

OPENING NOTES

A few months back, I paid a visit to Jackson Browne at his recording studio in Santa Monica. Over a long lunch, we talked about songwriting, guitars and his future plans. At one point, we were talking about, what else, surfing, and Browne informed me how his hobby found itself in one of his more recent songs. "Surfing is like a great metaphor for many other things. Especially the idea in surfing of being in the right place at the right time — to be at a beach when it's breaking, when it's not flat, to be in that part of the wave where it's all happening... it's very instructive about the rest of life."

Browne was referring to the tune "If I Could Be Anywhere," a great track he penned about the environment after a visit to the Galapagos Islands. But that "right place, right time" sentiment described my visit that spring day. Everything seemed to be "breaking" perfectly: the singer-songwriter just debuted his new signature model Gibson at NAMM, he was off the road just long enough to sit down and show off to us his very best guitars and — lest I forget — Browne's pals David Crosby and Graham Nash were in the main room of the studio, rehearsing. Yes, the pay sucks but sometimes my job does have perks.

As writer John Thomas accurately observes in this issue, Browne is quite possibly the ultimate guitar geek. He can write hit songs, he can sell out theaters and, yet, just like us guys with too much free time on our hands, he's still obsessing about the ultimate performance guitar, still daydreaming about what's next. Before I left his studio, he enthusiastically showed off an Epiphone Olympic he just bought after hanging out with David Rawlings (you know, the model we featured back in *FJ* #18).

Larry Pogrebra — the world's foremost expert on building hubcap resonator guitars *and* bowling ball canons — lives a unique existence. The former sidecar motocross racer (yes, that's a sport) alternates between off-the-grid homes in Montana and New Mexico building guitars that truly look and sound one-of-a-kind. Coincidentally, there's a Browne connection here: Along with Bonnie Raitt, Browne's sideman extraordinaire David Lindley is a proud Pogreba owner. Doc Simpson's visit to Willow Creek, Montana shows the builder in his native habitat, surrounded by plenty of toys, great guitars and the raw materials for many more of both.

There's another unplanned Browne connection. You'd never guess it from the jazz standards and his perfectly tailored suits, but guitarist John Pizarrelli cites Jackson Browne as a huge influence ... *and* Johnny Winter *and* Peter Frampton! So much for judging a book by its cover. Writer Rich Kienzle does a great job telling us how this rock 'n' roll kid became one of the world's great jazz guitarists. I just feel bad for the headstock of that Moll archtop!

Having famous musicians (or luthiers) interview each other has been one of our cornerstones from day one. There's a chemistry between artists just talking shop. In this issue, we mix up our formula and have Charlie Hunter talking with guitar builder Jeff Traugott. If your take on hot rodding a guitar is new strings and bridge pins, you'll be in for a shock. These guys are literally building a Winchester Mystery House of a guitar. And I don't think they're done tweaking it just yet.

Lastly, in response to all those who can't get enough of *the Journal*, we happily invite you to surf on over to fretboardjournal.com and check out our relaunched website. There, you'll find free Classifieds where you can buy and sell your coveted guitars and gear, lively blogs, interviews and podcasts galore with even more legends, even some outtakes from our print articles. On our page right now there's an exclusive video performance of "Something Fine" from Browne on his trusty old Gibson Roy Smeck. Share it with friends and consider it our little gift to you for supporting this unique magazine.

JASON VERLINDE
PUBLISHER

The Guitarist's

By *the Fretboard Journal* STAFF

We're generally opposed to list making in favor of deeper journalism, but the *FJ* couldn't resist this one: 99 things that we think every guitarist should do before they die. We posted the list on fretboardjournal.com in March and have already received a ton of responses on our site. Now you can have it on paper for posterity (and with handy check-off boxes to mark your progress).

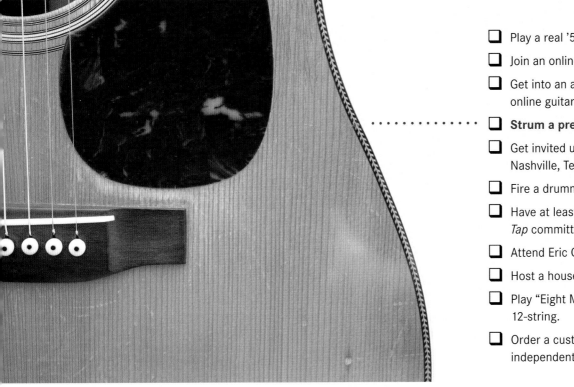

- ❏ Play a real '59 Gibson Les Paul Standard.
- ❏ Join an online guitar forum.
- ❏ Get into an argument with someone on an online guitar forum.
- ❏ **Strum a pre-war Martin herringbone.**
- ❏ Get invited upstairs at Gruhn Guitars in Nashville, Tennessee to see the good stuff.
- ❏ Fire a drummer.
- ❏ Have at least two quotes from *This is Spinal Tap* committed to memory.
- ❏ Attend Eric Clapton's Crossroads Festival.
- ❏ Host a house concert.
- ❏ Play "Eight Miles High" on a Rickenbacker 12-string.
- ❏ Order a custom guitar from an independent luthier.

Bucket List

- Pay for a neck reset.
- Buy a ukulele in Hawaii.
- Have a moment of twang on an original Blackguard Telecaster.
- Stick a mirror in your acoustic guitar's sound hole to look at the bracing.
- Attend a NAMM show, the annual trade show for musical instrument manufacturers held in Anaheim, California.
- Own a guitar worth more than your daily driver.
- Find yourself in a strange neighborhood chasing a Craigslist lead.
- See B.B. King perform.
- Swear off a particular brand of strings.
- Go to the Hardly Strictly Bluegrass Festival in San Francisco, one of the world's great music festivals (and it's completely free).
- Film yourself playing and post it on YouTube.
- Introduce yourself to one of your guitar heroes after a concert.
- Order a flight case to keep your favorite instrument safe and sound.
- Teach a kid his/her first three chords.
- Install a humidity gauge somewhere in your house.
- Change a broken string onstage in the middle of your set.
- Walk around Greenwich Village in New York City contemplating Bob Dylan and step into Matt Umanov's store.
- Attend a show at the Ryman Auditorium in Nashville, Tennessee.

- Travel to Paracho, Mexico, to see the world's only community centered around guitar building and order a nylon stringed model to take home.
- Play "Wipe Out" through a spring reverb.
- See a show at McCabe's Guitars in Santa Monica, California.
- Play a show at McCabe's Guitars in Santa Monica, California.
- Attend a guitar-centric summer camp such as Jorma Kaukonen's Fur Peace Ranch or the Puget Sound Guitar Workshop.
- Listen to Leo Kottke tell a joke between songs at one of his concerts.
- Take a class at the Old Town School of Folk Music in Chicago.
- Take a long roadtrip listening to Ry Cooder's *Paris, Texas* soundtrack.
- **Collect a vintage set of strings for the cool packaging, even though you have no intention of ever using them.**
- Hold a blacklight up to a vintage guitar to see if it's had any finish work done.
- Install a boutique set of pickups by yourself.
- Buy a cheap acoustic guitar specifically for outdoor jams and barbeques.

- ☐ Perform a song you wrote at an open mic.
- ☐ Play James Taylor's "Fire and Rain" on an Olson guitar.
- ☐ Buy a pick that costs more than $20.
- ☐ Lend a piece of expensive gear to a musician far more proficient than you.
- ☐ **Hoard a stash of tone woods for a custom guitar that you haven't fully decided upon yet.**
- ☐ Play through a tape echo.
- ☐ Attend a multi-day bluegrass festival like MerleFest or Telluride; partake in too much music and other stuff.
- ☐ Carry more than $5,000 in cash to a vintage guitar show, just in case something catches your eye.
- ☐ Play a little Robert Johnson on a 1920s or '30s Gibson L-00 or L-1.
- ☐ Talk about vintage Martin guitars with expert Richard Johnston of Gryphon Stringed Instruments in Palo Alto, California.
- ☐ Play Django Reinhardt's "Minor Swing" on a Selmer-style guitar.
- ☐ Peruse the halls of the Montreal Guitar Show, a giant showcase of the world's best lutherie held every July during the Montreal Jazz Festival.

- ☐ Burn yourself on a hot vacuum tube.
- ☐ Busk.
- ☐ Find yourself backstage at a stadium rock concert.
- ☐ Play a Collings at Quincy's Guitars in Austin, Texas.
- ☐ Learn how to Travis pick.
- ☐ Visit the Country Music Hall of Fame in Nashville, Tennessee.
- ☐ Refuse to buy an otherwise great guitar because you don't like the way the neck feels.
- ☐ Have Westwood Music's Fred Walecki captivate you for at least an hour with storytelling and guitars.
- ☐ Drop your guitar and then realize it's not the end of the world.
- ☐ Learn the middle and end of "Stairway to Heaven."
- ☐ Capture a Les Paul Monday at the Iridium in New York City (bonus points if you actually saw Les Paul play when you could).
- ☐ Try to play a harp guitar.
- ☐ Adjust a truss rod without any outside help.
- ☐ Play a vintage Weissenborn.
- ☐ **Take a factory tour at C.F. Martin & Co in Nazareth, Pennsylvania.**
- ☐ Attempt to play "Dueling Banjos" on a 5-string banjo.

- [ ] Force your family to visit Buffalo Brothers and take a Taylor Guitars factory tour on your San Diego vacation.
- [ ] Grow your fingernails out.
- [ ] Own Harry Smith's *Anthology of American Folk Music*, the influential boxed set of early blues and old-time music.
- [ ] Build your own cigar box guitar.
- [ ] Find your inner bluesman by taking a pilgrimage to the Crossroads Monument in Clarksdale, Mississippi, where Highways 61 and 49 meet.
- [ ] Learn an open tuning.
- [ ] Buy a 12-string guitar.
- [ ] Go to Elderly Instruments in East Lansing, Michigan, and ask to see the Tone Balls.
- [ ] Buy a short-scale or parlor guitar specifically for travelling.
- [ ] **Play a Carter Family tune on an old 16" Gibson L-5 like Maybelle's.**
- [ ] Find yourself on the Staten Island Ferry holding an instrument you just purchased from Mandolin Brothers.
- [ ] Scratch and sniff a piece of Brazilian rosewood.
- [ ] Go to the Rock and Roll Hall of Fame in Cleveland, Ohio.
- [ ] Conduct a photo shoot with your current guitar quiver.
- [ ] Own at least one guitar made in Kalamazoo, Michigan.
- [ ] Own at least one guitar made in Fullerton, California.
- [ ] Visit the Cavern Club in Liverpool.
- [ ] Learn a song written by a musician who is 15 years younger than you.
- [ ] Learn a song written by a musician who died before you were born.
- [ ] Restring your guitar in "Nashville" tuning.
- [ ] Play "Little Wing" on a Strat loud enough to upset the neighbors.
- [ ] Go look at the Stradivarius guitar at the National Music Museum at the University of South Dakota in Vermillion.
- [ ] Catch a set by Telecaster whiz Redd Volkaert at Austin's Continental Club.
- [ ] Regret that you sold a great guitar when you were younger and needed the cash.
- [ ] Learn the difference between a Duolian and a Triolian.
- [ ] Contemplate buying a guitar made the year you were born.
- [ ] Own an effects pedal not carried by Guitar Center.
- [ ] Miss a day of work because you were up too late playing.
- [ ] Write a song for your significant other.
- [ ] Subscribe to *the Fretboard Journal*.

So, how many have you done? Go to fretboardjournal.com/bucket and let us know.

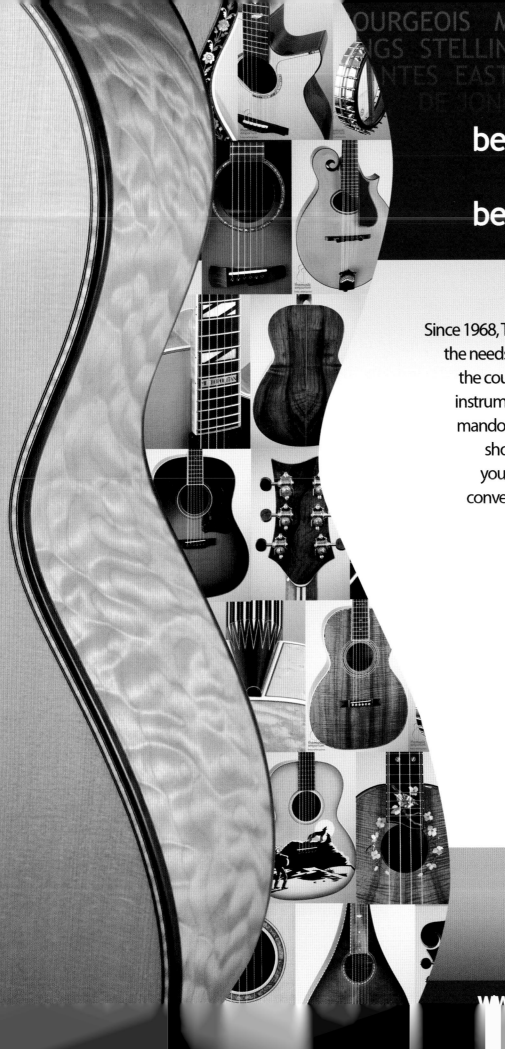

Triple Play

Three consecutive serial numbered 1937 Tonk Bros. Washburns

THE WASHBURN BRAND was launched by the giant musical goods distributor Lyon & Healy in the 1880s. Lyon & Healy sold many thousands of Washburn instruments through the first part of the 20th century, with mandolins and banjos accounting for a good amount of their early production. As guitar sales continued to grow in the late 1920's, the company built more Washburn flattop guitars, often of the smaller sizes popular during that era. But the Washburn line offered more than just parlor-sized guitars, including the "Lakeside Jumbo" model described in Lyon & Healy's 1912 catalog as a guitar made for steel strings that was 16-1/4" across the lower bout, 20-1/2" long, and with a body depth of 5-1/4". These dimensions are very similar in size to a modern day dreadnought, yet the Lakeside Jumbo

was introduced five years before the Ditson Company's earliest dreadnought models, and nearly 20 years before Martin's first dreadnoughts were first cataloged.

Founded in 1893, the Chicago based Tonk Bros. Co. was the Midwest's largest distributor of musical instruments and accessories when it acquired the Washburn brand from Lyon & Healy in 1928. Tonk offered Washburn instruments until production ceased at the onset of World War II, but as primarily a wholesale distributor, Tonk Bros. was never involved in the manufacturing of these instruments. Instead they contracted production to a few of the various manufacturing companies operating in or near Chicago at that time. Most vintage guitar experts agree that Washburn guitars

It's a family reunion you won't find on daytime talk shows. Here are three consecutive serial numbered Washburns, not seen together since they left the factory in 1937. Serial number 3244 is in the middle of the photo on the opposite page, 3243 is left and 3245 is on the right.

JASON VERLINDE

from the late 1920s until about 1940 were made by the Regal Musical Instrument Company in Chicago and the Gibson Mandolin-Guitar Mfg. Company in Kalmazoo, Michigan. Many of the higher grade Washburn models were constructed with great skill and using the best materials available at that time. A 1930s guitar chord book found in the case with a 1937 Washburn had hand-written notes on the cover stating that "Martin, Gibson and Washburn are the best brands." In about 1940, Tonk Bros. discontinued the Washburn brand, and the name remained unused until the '70s.

The 1937 Tonk Bros. catalog features the Washburn guitar line prominently. Included is the Regal made "Solo Model," which was labeled a "Large Auditorium" size guitar. The Solo was offered as a Model 5246 with rosewood sides and back and as a Model 5244, with mahogany sides and back. These guitars had solid "Eastern" spruce tops, ebony fretboards and the trademark Washburn "smile" shaped ebony bridge. They were fitted with early-pattern firestripe celluloid pickguards, Kluson "professional type nickel plated individual patent pegs" and "pearl inlaid head pieces." The necks are seven-piece laminations of mahogany and walnut with deep pronounced V carves, 25.4" scale length, and nut widths of 1-3/4 inches to 1-13/16 inches. The bodies of these guitars measure 15-1/2" wide at the lower bout and have deep sides, akin to Gibson's Jumbo model

Long before Stratabond, Washburn put a seven-piece neck on these Solo model guitars. Needless to say, they're still holding strong.

JASON VERLINDE

introduced in 1934, tapering from 4-3/4" to just under 4" at the heel of the neck.

With a soundhole diameter of 3-3/4", tiny bridge, deep body, long-scale neck and double-X unscalloped top bracing, the 5246 is a guitar with a distinctive voice. Big and bold, these instruments tend to have a strong fundamental tone and a very present mid-range response. The extra air volume and small soundhole aperture create an underlying sub-bass response that is noticeable across the strings, while the un-scalloped braces allow the trebles to have much more punch than one would expect from a big guitar. These are exceptionally versatile guitars, perfectly suited to flatpicks or fingertips.

Exclusively for *the Fretboard Journal* and courtesy of the author and Folkway Music in Guelph, Ontario, Canada, here are three beautiful examples of Tonk Bros.-era Washburn "Solo" Model 5246 guitars with consecutive serial numbers — together again for the first time since they left the workbench in Chicago back in 1937! Serial number 3244 in the middle of the opening photo has had a few modifications over the last 74 years, while #3243 on the left and #3245 on the right, are beautifully intact originals.

These are exceptionally rare guitars, and if not for the powers of the internet and the whims of the *Journal*, there is little chance the trio would have ever come to meet again.

— **Mark Demaray**

A TRADITION IN TONE.

A tradition born of 57 years of old world craftsmanship
and the finest materials, in the skilled hands of builders
dedicated to the unique quality and tone of Guild guitars.

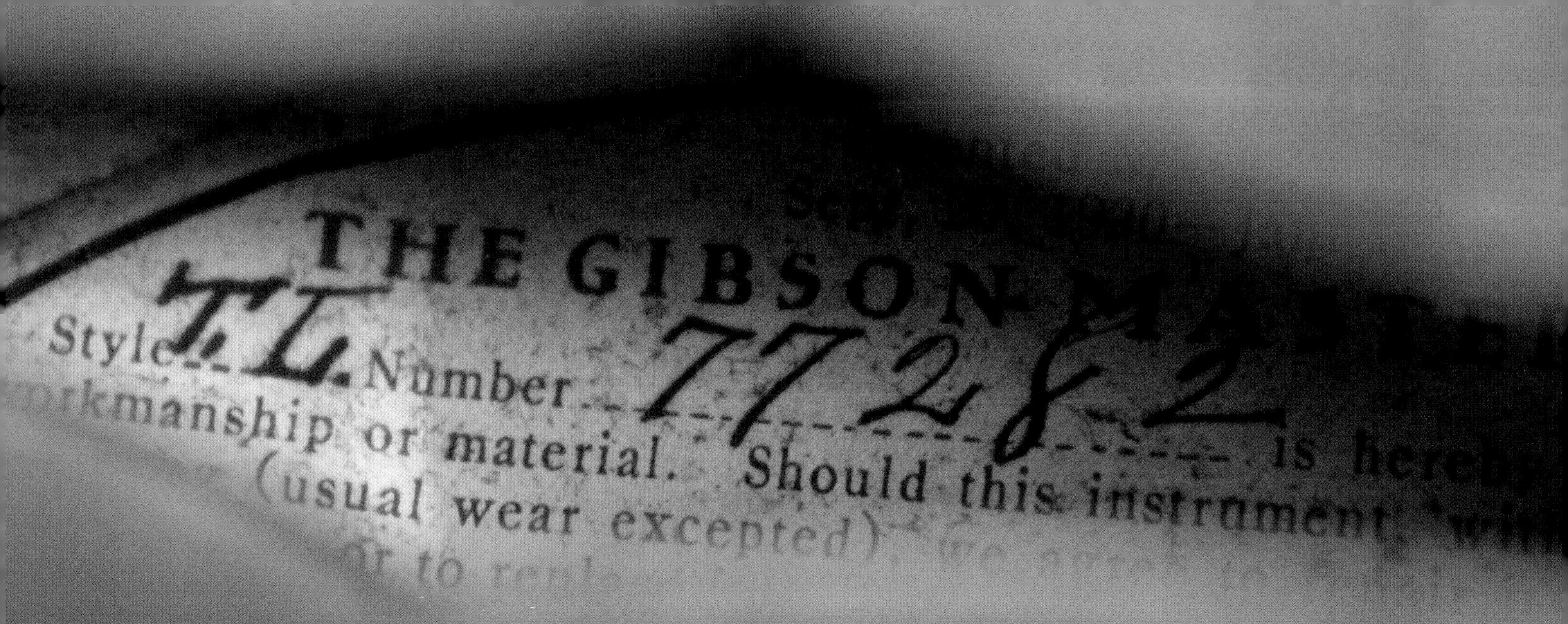

THE GIBSON
Style TL. Number 77282
Workmanship or material. Should this instrument
(usual wear excepted)

DURING HIS TENURE AT GIBSON from 1919 to 1924, Lloyd Loar oversaw the creation of such legendary instruments as the L-5 guitar and the F-5 mandolin, instruments that inspired musicians like Bill Monroe, Eddie Lang and Maybelle Carter to ever greater heights of musical innovation. On the other hand, Loar was also at Gibson for the creation of the tenor lute, an instrument that has done little more than inspire confusion and bafflement.

Looking back, you can sort of see what Loar and the Gibson were trying to do. In the early 1920s, the four-string banjo's popularity was increasing while the mandolin's was declining. The idea of sticking a tenor banjo neck on a mandolin-family body was an attempt to lure banjo players into the mandolin camp. The problem was, the tenor lute just didn't sound very good. The lightweight tenor banjo strings didn't have enough tension to drive the top efficiently, and consequently tenor lutes have a thin, anemic tone with not much volume.

Gibson offered the tenor lute for a couple of years, although most of the instruments that have survived seem to have been made in 1924. There were three versions made: the TL (pictured here), a similarly styled model with eight strings and an eight-string sunburst version called the TL-4. In case you were wondering, the eight-string models don't sound any better.

No one knows exactly how many tenor lutes were made, but most informed guesses put the number at under a hundred. The most annoying thing about the tenor lute is that it has a pear-shaped mandola body with f-holes, a configuration that never actually existed on Loar-era mandolas. More than one player has been tempted to convert a tenor lute to a mandola, but as near as I can tell, no one has taken the plunge yet.

— **Michael John Simmons**

The slender neck of the Tenor Lute doesn't have an adjustable truss rod, even though Gibson invented the now ubiquitous feature in 1922. This meant that the neck of the Tenor Lute is too flexible to be strung up with the heavier strings that would have made it sound better. *Inset:* The Tenor Lute's engraved tailpiece was a standard feature on Gibson's mandolins at the time.

The elegant "moccasin" headstock with the classic "The Gibson" inlay was standard on Gibson's mid-1920's banjos.

STYLE 1 / STRIPED MACASSAR EBONY / SINKER REDWOOD / GREEN HEART ABALONE
DESIGNED FOR ACOUSTIC VIBES MUSIC, TEMPE, ARIZONA

R Taylor

Taking guitars personally.

rtaylorguitars.com

Jailhouse Hula

WILLIAM STEDMAN'S HAWAIIAN GUITAR

AWHILE BACK I GOT A CALL from my good friend (and great guitar player/ songwriter) Don Bray. His friend, Devin Rehm, had inherited an old Hawaiian guitar from a family member. I was expecting a Weissenborn-made instrument or a Hilo Hawaiian — both of which are not so uncommon, even up here in Toronto.

When Don showed up at my shop with the guitar, I was completely bowled over by this behemoth of a thing he had under his arm. It had strings and it was guitar shaped, but I'd never seen anything from this gene pool. What struck me was how large it was. The lower bout measured a full 15-3/4" and the body at the endpin was 5-1/2" deep. It was like a Nick Lucas on steroids.

The guitar was full of idiosyncratic details. It had a tiny sound hole, a fully carved, huge round neck with a typical slotted headstock and period style three-on-a-plate tuners. The bridge was a curious design and it had a pickguard cut from some very thin ivoroid sheetstock. The pickguard material could have been salvaged from an old accordion covered in ivoroid.

But what really got my attention was down inside the sound hole: Suspended about two and a half inches down from the three piece pine top was a thin plate of wood with cutouts, looking a lot like a Virzi tone producer found on old Gibson mandolins.

I was getting really curious about this Hawaiian guitar and I needed more info. Don called on Devin to see if anyone in his family could fill in some of the

blanks; Devin contacted me with some details. The guitar was built sometime between 1920 and 1924 by William Stedman. (Devin's aunt Doris is married to Jim Stedman, William Stedman's grandson.)

It turns out Stedman was doing time in the Penetanguishene Penitentiary for murdering the man he caught messing with his wife. William Stedman was a gifted stone mason and during his prison term he was put to work building the stone wall around the penitentiary where he was incarcerated. It seems Stedman had solid transferable skills; he went from stone work to wood work with ease.

The Hawaiian guitar he crafted in prison over eighty years ago didn't need much to put it back into working order. I re-glued the bridge and filled the bolt holes in the bridge with bone. It needed a new bone saddle and nut, as well as new bridge pins. I cleaned it up and put on a fresh set of strings.

I was surprised at the lower volume coming from that big body, it might be due to the ladder bracing, nonetheless it had a very pleasant full warm tone, more like a flat top… a lot different from the sparkly overtones and sustain of Weissenborn-style instruments. No surprise, as this Hawaiian is radically different from anything I've encountered.

In addition to the one Hawaiian guitar and the stone wall that he built, apparently William Stedman also managed to build a mysterious mandolin during his Penetanguishene stint. The family has no idea of its whereabouts and it has yet to surface.

— Joe Yanuziello

Mother *of* PEARL

Kathy and Jimmi Wingert make guitars a family business

INTRODUCTION
BY MICHAEL
JOHN SIMMONS

PHOTOS COURTESY OF
WINGERT GUITARS

I'VE ALWAYS BEEN FASCINATED to discover how and why people become luthiers. One almost universal truth I've noticed is that the children of luthiers don't become luthiers themselves. There are a few cases, such as Canada's de Jonge family, that buck the trend, but they are few and far between. Perhaps only a luthier's kid knows just how much time and effort it takes to make a living building guitars? I remember one builder told me that the great thing about being a guitar builder is that you get to work half days. What you do with the other 12 hours is up to you.

The story of Jimmi Wingert, the up-and-coming inlay artist who is the daughter of acclaimed builder Kathy Wingert, is another exception to the rule. Growing up, Jimmi saw just how hard guitar building was and, like any sensible person, she wanted no part of it. But the desire to create something beautiful with her own hands was ultimately too compelling to resist. She started doing some simple inlays for her mother in 2002 and, from that humble beginning, has earned a reputation as an inlay artist of rare skill and creativity. I talked to both Wingerts at their Southern California workshop to find out what it's like keeping the craft of building and decorating guitars in the family.

Jimmi Wingert's modern take on the classic Celtic knot motif makes a lovely rosette on one of her mother's guitars.

Jimmi Wingert at her drawing table working out the intricate pattern for the inlay on the previous page.

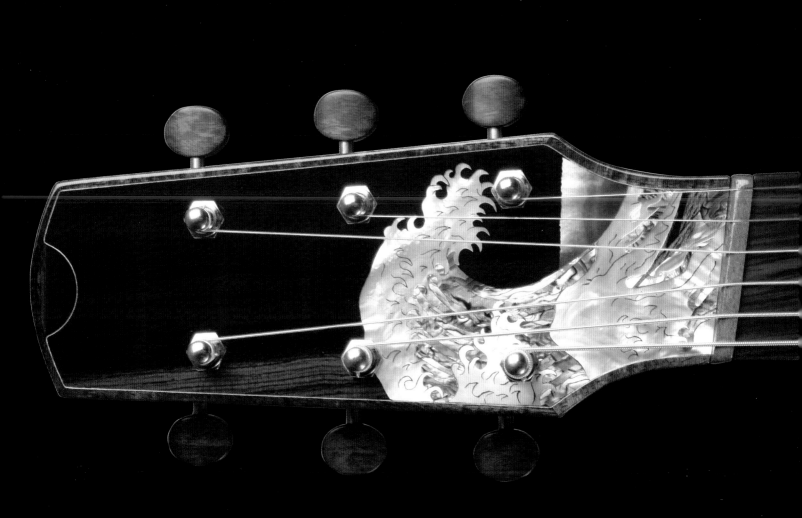

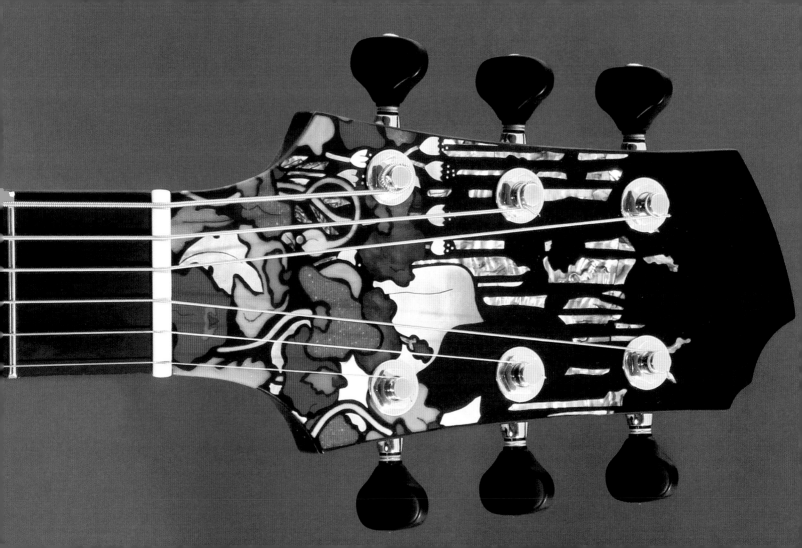

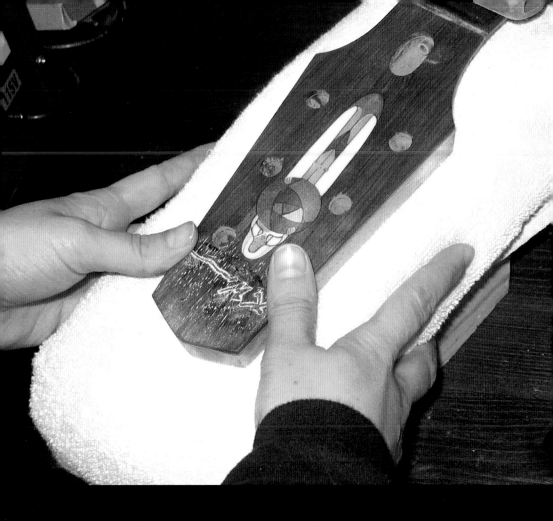

Gerald Sheppard. Mom is very supportive of other builders and encourages me to take on as many projects as I can, even if it cuts into her time. I've been around the guitar building process for so long I kind of know how to handle people's construction techniques and what to be careful about so they have plenty of material to work with. If I ever have a question about an approach she's always there for a consultation.

Kathy: One of the advantages of having me in the same workshop is that I come from a repair background as well as a building one. Each builder may have a different approach for parts that will

Jimmi: Right now I do everything by hand. Because it allows me to be really picky with the materials I use, I can get intricate designs with a flow. Judy Threet, the fabulous Canadian builder, gave me some great advice. She looks for patterns in the shell that she incorporates into the inlay design; sometimes she changes the design or builds around something that she sees in the shell. So I try to do that too, to look at the figure in the pearl and try to figure out what it wants to be. I greatly appreciate that tip from her.

At this point, pretty much every inlay I do is different with the exception of signatures and some of the designs that Mom created and that

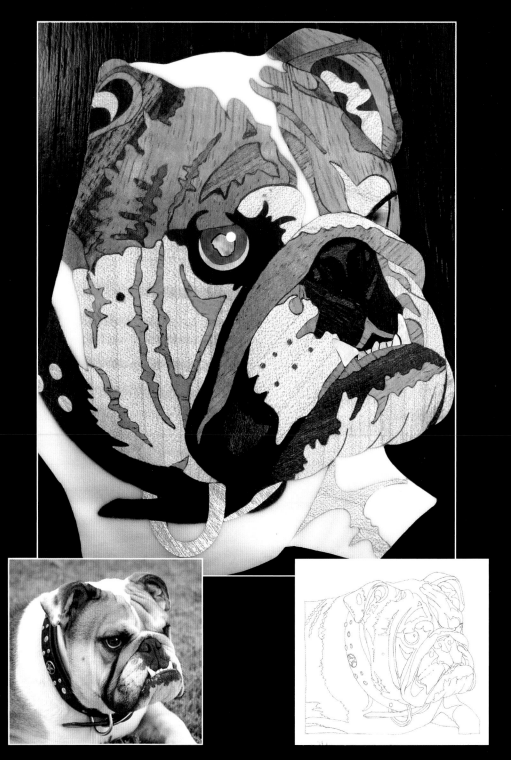

"This was done for one of Tim McKnight's customers," Wingert says. "The model is my English bulldog Driver, who spends a lot of time at the workshop. This is a great example of why I like sharing a workshop with my mother. All of the wood I used came from her scrap pile. I used koa, maple, mahogany, ebony and some dark mystery wood. His teeth and eyes are pearl and the white part of his body is Corian, that same stuff they make kitchen counters out of."

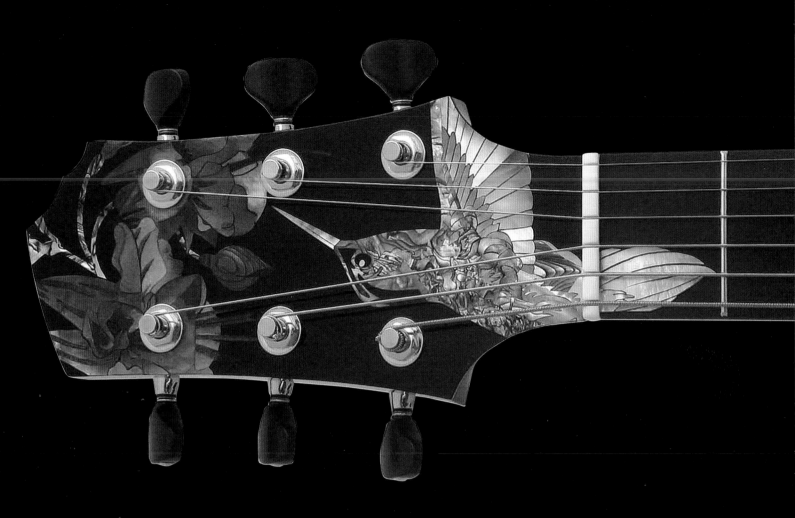

just have an idea. That said, a CNC machine would be helpful for the repetitive pieces like the big vines where many of the pieces are the same basic size and shape.

Kathy: The individual stuff — the portraits, the birds, the bulldogs and the art ideas — just can't be replicated by machine; every element has to be carefully hand-chosen, every piece leveled and smoothed and nit picked so the figure doesn't get lost. Jimmi excels at those designs.

Jimmi: If it were up to me, I would choose to stick with natural materials. But for the specific designs or pictures that people want, sometimes I have to go outside of natural materials and find things like plastics or reconstituted stone to get the color. I like to work with wood inlays, but it has its pros and cons. It's nice to cut, but it breaks really easily. I don't get as tired cutting it out by hand, but then I have to be really careful with it, 'cause it could snap if I'm not careful.

Another advantage of working with my mom is I get all of her little scrap pieces of wood to paw through. Sometimes I even like to think about what inlay I would do for myself if I had the free time, but it usually ends up on somebody else's guitar. I have a little electric guitar body that I was going to piece together, and I've been thinking about just inlaying the whole thing… 🪕

"This was an interesting experiment," Wingert says. "The fuchsias are actually two layers. I inlaid figured mother-of-pearl and then overlaid that with thin sheets of colored plastic. It doesn't really come across in the photo, but in person they just shimmer. I spent forever looking for just the right piece of abalone heart for the hummingbird's body. I wanted something that looked like feathers but that also had the contour of the bird's body. Inlaying birds and other animals can be very difficult. Usually the customer really knows the creature and I hear about it if I get any of the anatomical features wrong."

JAZZ GREAT

JOHN PIZZARELLI

UPHOLDS THE

FAMILY TRADITION

BY RICH KIENZLE
PHOTOGRAPHY BY JOHN PEDEN

Dynasty

$\mathcal{P}$ITTSBURGH'S OMNI WILLIAM PENN HOTEL is nearly a century old. There's live music in the huge, opulent lobby laden with fancy furniture, lavish draperies and huge crystal chandeliers. When I find John Pizzarelli, in a much more austere room, his slightly road-worn Moll Pizzarelli II seven-string is close by.

The Omni is serving as home for the John Pizzarelli Quartet during their four-day engagement at the Manchester Craftsmen's Guild. During our two-hour conversation, Pizzarelli recalls a youth where his love of rock peacefully coexisted with family jazz traditions. He can still remember the joys of discovering Nat King Cole, João Gilberto and other musical role models.

Pizzarelli's fan base spans generations, thanks to his engaging personality, smooth vocals and a repertoire that blends swing, the Great American Songbook and Brazilian fare with original songs and even the occasional nod to his rock and pop heroes. True, his dazzling guitar skills reflect the influence of his father, seven-string master Bucky Pizzarelli, but he is also known to add a few twists, including unison scat singing during his high-velocity solos — a trick he cheerfully admits lifting from George Benson.

Opinionated about guitars, music and his own recordings, Pizzarelli strikes a more reflective tone when discussing decades of performing with family, including his wife, the singer, songwriter and Broadway actress Jessica Molaskey. Pizzarelli may reside in Manhattan and perform worldwide, yet his priorities — family, music — and those New Jersey roots are unswayable.

Previous Spread: John Pizzarelli plays a Kala uke given to him by his manager, Joel Hoffner, alongside his daughter Maddie playing her Blue Ridge.

Jersey Boys

Bucky and Ruth Pizzarelli had a pair of daughters, Anne and Mary, before John Paul Pizzarelli made his entrance, on April 6, 1960, in Paterson, New Jersey, birthplace of his father — and of Frank Sinatra. The family lived in Clifton before moving to nearby Saddle River in 1963, the birth year of youngest son, Martin,

John's longtime bassist.

Bucky was an A-list Manhattan studio guitarist from the '50s into the '70s, playing on pop, jazz, rock and even country sessions. He was part of NBC's *Tonight Show* orchestra for several years at 30 Rock. He played his own jazz dates and made his own recordings, and he also spent 20 years recording and touring with swing legend Benny Goodman.

"We always joke that in our family, nobody plays 'Twinkle, Twinkle, Little Star' or 'Happy Birthday,'" John laughs. Mary, he says, can play Bix Beiderbecke tunes like "In the Dark" or "In a Mist" on the piano, as well as Billy Strayhorn's "Lush Life." Under Bucky's tutelage, Mary became proficient enough on guitar to record the 1932 Carl Kress-Dick McDonough jazz duet "Chicken a la Swing" with her dad. Anne plays piano, too, and reads music very well.

John's musical memories begin around 1964. "I vaguely remember seeing the Beatles on TV, [on] *Ed Sullivan*, my sister havin' those records, and I remember playing those records a lot — scratchin' them up and drawin' on the covers." Regarding his father's Beatles perspective, he notes, "I think the one thing he disliked was the volume, but he didn't mind the music, I don't think. He ended up playing a lot of those songs."

The younger Pizzarelli remains an unabashed Beatles fan. "The sounds of the guitars, the way they were used and just the general recording is so great, too," he says. "The way the drums sound, where the drums are located, where the guitars are located, and the idea of the 12-string guitar and the regular guitar and the acoustic guitar, the micing of the acoustic guitar on the *Abbey Road* record. I call my friend at Southern Illinois University, Rick Haydon, saying, 'I'm gonna buy that damn Rickenbacker 12-string...' But I never buy one."

Bucky Pizzarelli made a lot of rock records. ("He knew all those Brill Building songwriters," John says.) Dion and the Belmonts' "Teenager in Love," Dion's "Runaround Sue," Ben E. King's "Stand by Me,"

The artist's seven string Moll Pizzarelli Model II archtop. The guitar is 16" wide at its lower bout, just like an old Gibson L-5.

"My Moll is chewed up on the headstock, because when you drop off your guitar at airports now, they shush you away while they open it and never take any care in putting anything back in it's correct spot," Pizzarelli says. "The patch chord clips away the varnish and wood."

Ray Charles' "Georgia on My Mind," Del Shannon's "Runaway" and Frank Sinatra's "Fly Me to the Moon" are among the many rock and pop hits on which Bucky played. In 1975, John even heard his father on a hit of the moment: Janis Ian's "At Seventeen."

Fretted instruments always packed the Pizzarelli home. Among them were two D'Angelicos, Gretsch

Paramount tenor banjo, "with a leather head on it. It was stolen out of the house. I ended up with my uncle's Vega banjo, a nice old Vega."

Bobby Domenick played guitar in Bob Chester's orchestra, and in the early 1940s, Bucky watched him rehearse with a Paterson combo led by blind singer-accordionist Joe Mooney, who later led one of the

"Johnny Winter was the destroyer!"

seven-string models, ukuleles, a Fender Jazzmaster, an Ampeg Jet amp and a tweed Fender Tremolux that John later used. He also remembers two classical guitars and a couple of Gretsch 12-strings. "I don't know how the hell he got those," John says. "We had a Chet Atkins Super Axe I destroyed pretty good. He had a six-string Danelectro bass and six-string Fender bass, like John Lennon plays in the *Let It Be* movie."

Bucky's uncles, tenor banjoist Pete Domenick and his brother Bobby, who'd switched to guitar, shaped two generations of Pizzarellis. They tutored Bucky in the '30s; John followed in 1967. "I'd go to Victor's House of Music and take banjo lessons from Bobby," he recalls. Later, he studied with Pete. "My father would drive down to Pete's on Sunday. When my lessons were over, Bucky and Pete would play something. I never knew what they were playing. It was amazing." The Pizzarellis' *Sunday at Pete's* album, from 2007, honored both Domenicks and the tunes they learned from them.

"Pete had a really good system for learning songs, and I think it's been invaluable to playing rhythm guitar," John offers, "all the little things, chord-melody things. He made a tablature with numbers, and put how many strums, and then the melody note would be circled. You could learn 'Yes Sir, That's My Baby' and 'Bye, Bye Blues,' but you still learned chord names. And it was fun, because you learned songs at 7 years old, strummin' away." John used Bucky's vintage

great small groups in jazz. Today, John owns Bobby's Epiphone Emperor.

"When my uncle died, in '72, my aunt sold the guitar to some guy in North Carolina," he recalls. After a stroke sidelined the new owner, "he sold the guitar back to my dad for not a lot of money, and he gave it to me — a beautiful, great old guitar. It's got some cracks in it. It's very nice."

The Pizzarelli kids met jazz history up close and personally when Bucky's musician pals would visit his Saddle River home. Among the regulars: guitar wiz Joe Pass, swing violinist Joe Venuti, bassist Slam Stewart, saxophonist Zoot Sims and, notably, Les Paul, who lived in nearby Mahwah. Paul's visits were special to John, who used two cassette recorders to emulate his multitracking. "The thought that went into all that music was so amazing to me — hearing him tell the stories…"

Though John played trumpet in high school, a brief flirtation with piano lessons ended when, as he puts it, "the piano fired me." Baseball was a youthful passion, but "when I got to high school, I realized I wasn't that good. I wanted to play sports and music but I ended up in music."

Frampton to Hampton

At first, playing music meant playing the music of his generation.

"The banjo was my great uncle Pete's, given to me on my son's first birthday 20 years ago," Pizzarelli says. "It is a Vega with the same Gibson strings on it that he played. Still has the leather head on it, too. It's a beauty. Pete was my dad's teacher and taught me for a while until he died in 1972."

"I was a big Peter Frampton guy… a big Jackson Browne fan," John says. "James Taylor — I liked Danny Kortchmar's guitar work with him. I always loved the Steely Dan records, readin' the liner notes, seeing Larry Carlton and Rick Derringer's names on some of those. Johnny Winter was the destroyer! There was a live record of him playing 'Bony Moronie,' a great record. Robin Trower. There were a lot of guitar players I liked in those days."

Emanon ("no name" spelled backwards) launched John's rock-band phase in 1974. "I used [my father's] Fender Jazzmaster for a while. For Christmas, I got a Madeira solid-body made by Guild, and we put a DiMarzio pickup in the back. That was hilarious, because we got a guy to hook it up. Nobody [could] get it to stay in — couldn't get the right screw; we taped it in." Rehearsals in the family garage involved huge amps at high volume. ("Very loud," Bucky laughs today.) The volume sometimes brought the local police, whom they got to know on a first-name basis.

Still, Bucky's open-mindedness allowed for the father-son musical communication to be two-way. "I actually remember, on the out chorus of [Steely Dan's] 'My Old School,' Jeff Baxter played a lick — a lick I heard him play on a Doobie Brothers record later on — and I remember my father saying, 'What's that one? That's a good lick!' Right in the fadeout. So certain things he liked."

Hearing John and some friends play Chick Corea at a school talent show gave Bucky a stronger inkling about his son's ability. "He heard me play 'Spain' and said, 'How'd you guys learn all that stuff?' We said it was on the record. Bucky's response was, 'Here's Django Reinhardt, here's George Barnes — learn all this stuff!'" Bucky can remember a wager with his son involving Django Reinhardt's 1937 recording of "Rose Room," with the Quintet of the Hot Club of France. "I bet five bucks; I'd give him five bucks if he learned how to play it. And he learned this chorus."

"That's how I started to figure out some of the ins and outs of the jazz stuff," John says. "Single-note came from playing with my dad, but a lot was George Barnes." A versatile electric-guitar pioneer, Barnes made his name on records and radio in Chicago before becoming a top New York studio musician. From 1969 to 1972, he played in a duo with Bucky. "He's the unsung hero of the single-note guitar,"

Pizzarelli out of school!'" By 1980, he was out. "I worked the whole summer. I saved all my money, I worked at a day camp and I did gigs at night, because I wanted to record my demos with a real producer."

At camp, he met fellow counselor Mike Taplinger, who'd studied with Bucky's close friend, Manhattan

"I bought a Stratocaster in 1979. I think that's the one I hid under the bed for a while…"

John maintains. "He could play any style, and I think he still chops up the jazz guys. Just impeccable guitar playing."

In 1978, with high-school graduation looming, John began playing and singing in local restaurants. "Whether they listened or not, it didn't really matter," he remarks. He also started purchasing his own gear. "I bought a Stratocaster in 1979. I think that's the one I hid under the bed for a while — never let him know I had it, because Bucky was always mad I was buyin'. He'd say, 'What'd you buy *that* guitar for?'"

John certainly had his choice of weapons. "I had [the Strat] and the Atkins Super Axe Gretsch that had been given to me by my father. I used that for a while at the end of high school. I ended up getting a Fender Flame, a double cutaway — nice guitar, too. I had some good solidbodies over the years. I also bought a Mesa Boogie SOB Son of Boogie amplifier. You put the guitar at six, it's clean; at 10, it overdrives the amp. Great sound, but [it weighed] 9,000 pounds!"

Less weighty were his three unproductive semesters at the University of Tampa (majoring in trumpet) and two at Jersey's William Paterson University. "Everybody said, 'That's enough!'" he laughs. "School chancellors wrote and said, 'Get

rhythm-guitar master Barry Galbraith. Using one of his dad's seven-strings, John practiced with Taplinger and did a few gigs. "That's where I sort of learned seven-string guitar. My father'd say, 'Here's what you gotta do!'" With Dad playing by his side, John made his first commercial recording, *2 x 7 = Pizzarelli*, for New York-based Stash Records. *Swinging Sevens* followed in 1984.

Working with local singer Joe Francis in the late '70s, John became acquainted with a future vocal role model: Nat King Cole. The two King Cole Trio best-of LPs he bought, at Bucky's urging, introduced him to Cole standards he'd later record, not to mention guitarist Oscar Moore's skills as accompanist and soloist. He calls the Trio "beyond itself, beyond everybody else."

John's bifurcated musical career had him freelancing solo as well as gigging around Jersey and Manhattan with Bucky as a seven-string duo. "We worked together in the summer of 1980. I did Sundays solo, Mondays at Julio's with Joe Francis, then Tuesday through Saturday with Bucky — through the summer, workin' every night."

The shows with Bucky proved to be quite informative. "I learned everything on the Bucky gigs.

A vintage Epiphone Emperor formerly owned by Bobby Domenick. This guitar, and its owner, had a tremendous impact on the Pizzarelli clan. The archtop now belongs to John.

Just play melodies, and good luck! He'd just start to play and look at me. Eventually, I could sort of sense if he finished an A section in E flat, and the bridge went to G, he'd play a lick. You started to learn how songs worked. He would never say F7 or C7; he would just play. I'd say, 'Write the chords out, and I'll just follow you and I can hear the song.' He said, 'Ah, just listen to what I'm gonna play! I don't have to write anything out.'"

That type of training would come in handy — like, for instance, when John's trio played at an octogenarian couple's 50th anniversary party. "Somebody said, 'Grandpa's gonna sing a song now.' My piano player said, 'I don't know that song.' I said, 'I don't either, but I know I'm gonna know it.'" As the old man began singing, John knew exactly what was going to happen. "A song from the '20s — probably won't have a bridge. It'll probably be two 16s and a tag at the end. Sure enough, it was just like that. I sat around Bucky enough to know how these songs worked.

"It was a great thing that from 20 to 30, I was sittin' next to him, just listening. I used my ears all that time to hear changes — really developed a whole other arm for me, learning like that. That's how Joe Mooney did it, because he was blind. I'm sure that's one of the things [my dad] got from Joe."

Bucky, who recorded with Mooney in 1951, confirms that view. "Joe Mooney had no music. He got [his sidemen] together and dictated licks to each one of them. And all of a sudden, they played together, and it sounded like a symphony."

Solo Flight

Describing the contrasts between his style and that of his son, Bucky explains, "He sang at the same time, developed his single-string playing on his own, and he's got his own little style, which is good. He plays fast tempos — faster than I can play. He's got that rock background and a little of that comes out

once in a while. He knows how to do it."

Playing together onstage, John would pick one of Bucky's Benedetto seven-strings, while Bucky would use his Gretsch Van Eps model — both plugged into one Duovox accordion amp. Late in the summer of '80, they heard Brazilian guitarist João Gilberto on the car radio — it was the 1977 album *Amoroso* — a moment John calls the "beginning of bossa nova for me. Bucky got excited and said, 'Buy the record.' It's funny — January of 1980 was Nat Cole; August was *Amoroso*."

The younger Pizzarelli defines Brazilian guitar as "all about finding the bass note and chord, being able to walk it and play it. You see a good Brazilian play the chord; they make those open strings work just like country guys do. That's why the guitar is so beautiful in all those different phases. Somebody found a way to make it sound like an orchestra." Gilberto's style, he says, was "in the rhythm."

Meanwhile, drastically different rhythms were coming from Johnny Pick and His Scabs, John's rock band. With brother Martin on electric bass, they tackled tunes by Little Feat, the Allman Brothers and the Beatles, plus Beatle covers like Carl Perkins' "Everybody's Trying to Be My Baby" and Buck Owens' "Act Naturally." John used his Fender Flame. "I don't know how the hell we did three and a half hours, but it was fun."

Occasionally, John fronted the Scabs in a tux before leaving for a more lucrative gig with Bucky. Club owners resented him ducking out, but he wanted to play as much as he could. "I played anywhere and everywhere. If I could play with the rock band, I did. I made enough — it came out to $400 at the end of the week.

"That was the joke. I played jazz to support my rock 'n' roll habit."

Stash released *I'm Hip (Please Don't Tell My Father)*, John's first vocal album, in 1983. Backed by Bucky and his trio, he laid down 10 vocals, including Dave Frishberg's "I'm Hip," some Nat Cole, two

Source Material

A word with Bucky Pizzarelli

Bucky & John Pizzarelli, Burbank, CA, June 28th, 2005.

At 85, Bucky Pizzarelli has a schedule that would exhaust many younger musicians. When we met at Pittsburgh's Duquesne University in July of last year, he candidly discussed musical philosophies, talked of future plans and shared 1945 Army stories. Like the time the Philippines' oppressive heat and humidity unglued ("boiled," he says) his Gibson archtop in its case...

"I'm always thinking!" he says in reference to his current recording career. "After I finish an album, I'm working on another one right away." Diggin' Up Bones, from 2009, was credited to "Buck Pizzarelli and the West Texas Tumbleweeds," and it reflected Bucky's longtime admiration for country music; his sons John and Martin plus legendary Grand Ole Opry pedal-steel player Tommy White joined in the fun. "It was nerve-wracking about the country date," John Pizzarelli admits. "Martin's looking at me like, 'What are we doin' here?' Tommy was so good, sayin', 'You're in the right ballpark; you're cool.'"

Last year, the group (with pianist Monty Alexander included in the mix) recorded a second country set, which, John adds, was far easier. Bucky's latest solo album: exploring the music of '30s cornet giant Bix Beiderbecke — "with a string quartet," Bucky says. "Songs Bix was famous for: 'I'm Comin' Virginia,' 'Singin' the Blues,' all those things."

As a top session guitarist for decades, Bucky had to be an impeccable sight-reader, but otherwise, the niceties of music theory seem to mean little to him. "I think playin' the guitar, just your fingers on the fingerboard—that's the secret. Don't worry about namin' a chord 'G minor seventh with a flat five.' By the time you say it, it's past you. It's a crutch! Feel! You gotta look at your fingers and put them in the position where C is, where B flat is... "

He sees parallels between his own boyhood musical heroes and the Beatles' impact on John and other younger musicians. "The whole thing is being inspired by somebody," he explains. "I listened to Benny Goodman, Duke Ellington, Count Basie, Freddie Green. I said, 'I want to do that!' I aimed everything, all my knowhow, at playin' in the band." Asked why Green's 4/4 rhythm-guitar style is a lost art to young players, he responds, "They never heard it. That's the trouble. They don't listen!"

"I think it's a necessity to learn rhythm guitar, for anybody who wants to play guitar," Bucky continues. "Kids have to have an acoustic rhythm guitar, an electric guitar and a classical guitar. You gotta do all three!"

He's also emphatic that records aren't the ultimate arbiters of success. "When you learn a difficult piece, you've got it. The true test is when you play it in front of people, not when you're recording."

originals and two by Mooney, whose relaxed vocal style was also an influence. "We went in at 9 or 10 in the morning; by 5, I walked out with a cassette of 10 mixed songs from the record." Stash then released the vocal record *Hit That Jive, Jack!* in 1985 and *Sing! Sing! Sing!* two years later.

In 1989, New York-based Chesky Records signed John as a vocalist, and, backed by top Manhattan jazzmen, he recorded the album *My Blue Heaven* using one of Bucky's Benedettos. Chesky released *My Blue Heaven* in 1990, amid Harry Connick Jr.'s run of bestselling jazz-vocal albums for Columbia. RCA, anxious for their own Connick, signed Pizzarelli to their prestigious Novus jazz division. "To be the singer at that label was a big deal at that time," John says.

Around this time, he got one of his own Benedetto instruments. "I was going to get a Charlie Christian-Oscar Moore kind of guitar. My father said, 'Benedetto's got one for you!' Benedetto made me a plywood guitar — a laminated top, a very plain

plain blonde."

Following *New Standards* in 1993, the Nat Cole homage *Dear Mr. Cole* in 1994 and the live-to-two-track *After Hours* the following year, RCA upped the ante, assigning him to pop producer Ron Fair, who's since gone on to work with Christina Aguilera and, more recently, Lady Gaga. For 1997's *Let's Share Christmas*, Fair hired top jazz orchestral arrangers, including Don Sebesky, known for his work on some of Wes Montgomery's Verve and A&M albums.

Sebesky and Pizzarelli bonded creatively. For the album *Our Love Is Here to Stay*, the arranger gave "Honey Pie," Pizzarelli's first Beatles cover, a Count Basie-style big-band treatment. "Everybody asked about 'Honey Pie,'" John recalls. "I thought, They're 'wowing' over one [Beatle tune]; they'll 'wow' over 12!" Backed by RCA's U.S. head Bob Jamieson, Pizzarelli, with his Benedetto and Bucky's old Fender Tremolux, went on to record *John Pizzarelli Meets the Beatles*.

Sebesky wrapped various Fab Four standards in "classic jazz" styles, melding "Can't Buy Me

"That was the joke. I played jazz to support my rock 'n' roll habit."

guitar I could travel with. He made two laminates, and they were great!" John's self-produced *All of Me* (1991) utilized a big band on some tracks, strings and small-group accompaniment on others; he used his Benedetto on the album. 1992's *Naturally* proved more satisfying.

"The second record's better, because I knew how the band worked," he explains. "I knew where I wanted to [define] how the guitar was gonna exist on that record, so I wrote 'Seven on Charlie,' a takeoff on [Charlie Christian's] 'Solo Flight,' and I really worked the guitar in well. I had the laminate [Benedetto] for *Naturally* that I had gotten the previous summer, the

Love" with Woody Herman's big-band anthem "Woodchopper's Ball," and "Here Comes the Sun" with '60s-style bossa nova. For "Get Back," he re-created his famous Wes Montgomery orchestrations behind Pizzarelli's vocals. "I really thought the Beatle record was gonna be the cream of the crop," John says. "I thought, That'll put me over!"

It didn't quite happen that way.

During mixing, John discovered a massive philosophical disconnect with Fair, who'd been unable to attend the actual sessions. "There was always a scene, because he was a rock 'n' roll guy. He had the right idea, but he didn't know when to lay off. We

not in large sales, but when I'd go to Brazil, you play 'Can't Buy Me Love,' they stand on their feet. They loved it in Japan… everywhere but the United States." Pizzarelli's eight years with RCA ended soon after that.

Shifting Gear

The move away from RCA wasn't his only shift during the late 1990s. He also began playing and endorsing Springfield, Missouri, luthier Bill Moll and his custom guitars. "Bill's made me some great guitars, and we've had a lot of fun talking about guitars and designing," John says. He's never really explained why he made the switch, until now.

"You know the God's-honest reason? It's the first time I'll say it, and I'll probably regret it: I honestly felt like Bucky Pizzarelli was a Benedetto artist. My father did a lot of my negotiating, unbeknownst." John wasn't exactly asking his father for Benedetto guitars, but he would wind up with them anyway. "He said, 'I think Benedetto's got one — you should play that!'"

John is quick to laud Bob Benedetto's role in reviving interest in archtops. "Bob's a great guitar maker. Bob in 1980 was the first. We had the Blue Guitars [exhibit] at the Smithsonian, and everybody and his brother was makin' [archtops]." Moll, he explains, was "a struggling guitar guy" when they met. "He said, 'I'd love to make a guitar for you.' It's like we were contemporaries, and I said, 'Well, you know what? I would like that!'

"And Bob got mad. I just said, '[Moll] wants to make guitars for me.' Bob doesn't not talk to me or anything; he just was upset. I know I can go some [places], and I'm Bucky Pizzarelli's son — and that's fine, 'cause I am. It was no harm [intended]; I just felt Bob should be *Bucky's* guitar maker."

John now owns three Moll archtops. The first (the "Pizzarelli") is on the cover of *Let There Be Love.* "That's the orange one; then there's the brown one, which was a black one, which is hilarious. It's

spent a whole session fixing a drum thing. It's like, 'Why are you bothering? You're wasting money you don't have to spend!'"

Jamieson, too, was dissatisfied. "He said, 'You gotta get rid of "You Can't Do That." "Gotta Get You Into My Life" [has] gotta go. We need more guitar!' So we added 'Eleanor Rigby.' We did a cover of 'I Feel Fine' that never made the record, just the quartet. It was just swingin'."

RCA's shortsightedness ultimately doomed the album. "The idea was to attract a different listener to a style of music they wouldn't listen to through songs they knew. They got [the idea] all over the world —

an eggplant color now… [They're] two really great carved-tops I wouldn't take out of the house." The third, Moll's Pizzarelli Model II, is his road guitar, a laminate with Florentine cutaway he's used since about 2006.

"Sixteen inches wide, like an old Lloyd Loar [Gibson archtop]. Bill designed a tailpiece, and I wanted a smaller headstock, 'cause it fits better in a case. I said, 'How about a scalloped tail, just for laughs?' I'm really bad with my guitars… I keep my patch cord in the guitar, so when they take it out of the case, it gets all chipped up. But it's a hell of a box. It really is great acoustically. It has a nice, stable sound."

His classical models include one made by John Higgins in St. Louis and a very thin cutaway that Bill Moll built. "He's made me another, based on the Rubio classical design, same size — it's gorgeous." That instrument is equipped with an RMC bridge pickup. "It just looks like a classical guitar with a seventh string, and this pickup is really good."

In 2000, Pizzarelli signed with Cleveland-based audiophile label Telarc. "That first record, *Kisses in the Rain,* was fun to make," he remembers. "I said, 'We're going to make a trio record [with Martin and pianist Ray Kennedy].' It was 70 percent stuff we played on the road, so it was an easy record to make." Per Telarc's exacting audio standards, they recorded live, digitally, in the studio.

"It's a whole other method I've only just figured out two records ago," he admits. "It's nerve-wracking. You gotta be able to fix the voice no matter what you do. And the hard part is, you're playing and singing. So you make the compromise and say, 'It's good enough,' or I'll go back in and play and re-sing where I have to."

John's amplifier choices have varied. "Up to the Beatles [album], sometimes I just went direct. A lot of the time, I had a little Gallien-Krueger my dad had. I used a Peavey tweed on *Kisses in the Rain.*" For 2002's *The Rare Delight of You,* which teamed him with pianist Sir George Shearing and His Quintet,

he used an UltraSound.

Shearing, of course, has been internationally celebrated since the late 1940s for his cool bebop style, but this collaboration also had a deeper meaning for Pizzarelli, because sessions took place in Manhattan just a month after 9/11. "It just reaffirmed why we have music on the planet, especially with [George] sittin' right there." Working with Shearing guitarist Reg Schwager, says Pizzarelli, was "one of the few times we had a guitar player that wasn't related to me on the date. Reg was wonderful."

Following 2003's *Live at Birdland,* Pizzarelli augmented the trio with an assortment of Brazilian musicians and recorded *Bossa Nova,* which brought the guitarist a sort of personal validation. "To blow my own horn, the Brazilians reaffirmed that everything I learned listening to João Gilberto, I got right. It would have been really bad if I'd started to play, and they went, 'No, not so good.' They went, 'Beautiful, beautiful!' I was so happy I got it right. That was one of the records Telarc was ambivalent about. They said later, 'We'll be damned, that thing's still sellin'!'"

Soon after *Bossa Nova* was released, the trio became a quartet with the addition of drummer Tony Tedesco. (Pianist Larry Fuller replaced Kennedy in 2005.) Tributes to Richard Rodgers and Duke Ellington would follow. Recording the Ellington album last year at Manhattan's Nola Studios, John used his Pizzarelli II and the tiny JazzKat amp he endorses. Recording the guitar through several sources gave him multiple guitar sounds for any given passage.

"We were able to, in the mix, say, 'This part, I'd like more acoustic rhythm, and, next part, I'd like more of the electric sound. I was really pleased to get the kind of sound I get when I play live." Seeing computer-based home recording replacing actual studios, however, troubles him. "I like the studio," he asserts. "I like the goin'-to-work kind of idea."

Since his move to Telarc, his albums have continued to find an audience. "The first [Telarc

Larry Carlton's signature adorns the back of Pizzarelli's Larry Carlton signature model Gibson 335. "I did a gig honoring him at the Rock and Roll Hall of Fame and we had a great time playing together," Pizzarelli says. "I told him I was glad to get to play with him after all the sleep I lost trying to learn the 'Kid Charlemagne' solo as a kid. I call it my Spinal Tap guitar: You can't even look at it… don't touch it… don't look at it!"

album] did really well. They've all done between 50,000 and 65,000. When all's said and done, there are people that'd kill for those numbers. We've had a really good run on the Ellington record… I'm hopin' we'll get to make another for Telarc. I've been sayin' if I'd get to 100,000, I'd be happy. Diana Krall's people got mad because her big-band record only sold 500,000 or whatever. I'd kill for 500,000."

Pizzarelli remains outspoken about guitars, especially today's mass-produced, high-end models. "I think the custom guys are cuttin' them up, because I don't think they give the attention to the guitar player." Similar skepticism extends to low-priced import incarnations of iconic brands. "I think Russell Malone likes his D'Angelico. But… it won't be like [the originals] as they age. It's amazing, the sound of some of those old ones."

His string choices include La Bella seven-string tape-wounds — ".014 on the top to .079 on the bottom" — and he uses a Steve Clayton .94mm pick. "A guy gave it to me in St. Louis, and it was just the right amount of tension for me. Bucky plays the thin,

on the road, "They're easy to get, but trying to dial in a sound… I just like to see volume and bass and treble. I'll take midrange," he laughs, "but when you get to master, post-master and up-master, down-master, I don't know how to work them. That's why the JazzKat's good: doesn't have a lot of lows and highs — a nice, flat sound."

Roots to Branches

Today, John's children continue the Pizzarelli musical tradition. Johnny, his son from his first marriage, is a drummer; Maddie, his daughter with Molaskey, studies piano and dabbles in bass and guitar. "They have great minds and memorize things so fast." He marvels at the differences in how he heard music when he was growing up, as compared to what the web offers. "We sat down with [cassette] recorders; they just go *click, click, click*!"

As for brother Martin, he grew up around bass giants like Ray Brown, Slam Stewart, Milt Hinton and George Duvivier — all Bucky's friends. John calls him

"I learned everything on the Bucky gigs. Just play melodies, and good luck! He'd just start to play and look at me."

crummy picks. I like one with a little meat to it." He also touts his tiny solid-state JazzKat TomKat, equipped with a single tube and eight-inch speaker. "It's a lot of power. I can carry it around, mic it, take it direct. When I play in clubs, it's perfect — the right amount of low and high, so you get a nice, balanced sound. I wish I could figure a way to take it around the country with me."

As for the Fender Twin or Roland amps he uses

"a real, true bass player. He doesn't care about playin' solos. He wants to know where to play two, when to play four, what to do here, how to move the music. He re-harmonizes by instinct as opposed to knowledge, but the instincts are really good."

Family collaborations onstage and on record seem endless. John produces Molaskey's albums; everyone records with everyone else. 2009's freewheeling *PIZZArelli Party*, for example, included

Bucky, John, and Martin and added Molaskey plus violinist Aaron Weinstein, singer Rebecca Kilgore and tenor saxophonist Harry Allen — all members of the extended musical family. "Harry Allen and Aaron, we raised all these kids. It really makes for a delightful experience. In the studio, thinking about swing music, you couldn't have a more joyful noise. We get all excited about that."

Given his authentic roots, it's no surprise Pizzarelli is dismissive of zoot-suited "swing-revival" bands with "loud backbeats and bad rhythm-guitar players playin' barre chords... , horn lines all in unison." He does laud the ongoing popularity of Great American Songbook albums, noting, "People are buyin' this music in the millions, even the dumb Rod Stewart records!" While calling Stewart " a great rock 'n' roll singer," Pizzarelli downplays Stewart's standards albums as "a musical nightlight: straight line, no up and down, nothing loud, nothing soft."

On the other hand, he has a lot of respect for the country idiom. "I had the record *Chester & Lester* [by Chet Atkins and Les Paul]. I loved to hear Roy Clark when I could." He also praises Bob Wills. "It's swing music to me, you know? I liked Asleep at the Wheel, too."

Radio Deluxe, a syndicated weekly program on 70 stations nationwide, offers him a chance to share some of his favorite tunes. The show features Pizzarelli and Molaskey, in their Manhattan living room, blending playful repartee and special guests with a hyper-eclectic blend of music. "It's just a way to get to play Bob Dylan, Joni Mitchell, Count Basie, Ella Fitzgerald and our records. We try to educate in our own little way."

"I wish I could sell more records, to be honest with you," he says. "It would make my performing life easier. If I could sell 150,000 records, I could plan out my tours better, take the summer to be with my family and be able to say, 'September to here, January to there,' and know what I was gonna do.

"I mean, I'm not at all displeased," he continues.

"We've been lucky; we've never had to do anything we don't want to do. I've been able to do the records I want to make. I haven't sold 100,000, but I can look back at 20 records and say, for the most part, 'I could listen to these records.'"

For Pizzarelli, family and music still rule. He beams as he recalls a recent Christmas spent at his father's house.

"He'd hand me the L-5 and say, 'Play that one! Is that good?' Then he'd hand me the D'Angelico, and I'd play that. There was an Epiphone he liked. He loves restringing them, having me play 'em. He'd say, 'That one sounds good. Try this one!' It was Guitar 101 — figurin' out stuff and havin' fun." 🎸

BY MICHAEL JOHN SIMMONS

Engine Check

PHOTOGRAPHY BY RACHEL BLECKMAN

FIRST HEARD CHARLIE HUNTER about twenty years ago in a small club in Berkeley, California. I had heard rumors about a monstrously good guitarist who played a unique eight-string guitar/bass hybrid that sounded more like a Hammond organ that anything that was actually fretted, and I was intrigued. When I arrived at the club after a losing bout with the Bay Area traffic, Hunter was well into his first set. At first I was amazed by the sheer weirdness of his guitar. From my spot in the back of the room I tried to figure out how the eight strings were set up, what kind of pickups he was using, what all those knobs and switches did and all the other guitar geek questions that inevitably fill my mind when faced with a new species of fretted instrument. But those questions quickly faded from mind as I was overwhelmed by Hunter's musicality.

As advertised, he was an amazingly adept technician, but after a few moments I forgot about that and spent the rest of the evening happily adrift in an intensely rhythmic, soulful wash of sound. During the break I wandered to the front of the stage to get a closer look at Hunter's guitar and saw that it was indeed a guitar/bass hybrid. The bass section, which was strung with real honest to goodness bass strings, consisted of three strings while the guitar section had five strings. I learned that his instrument was made by the Oakland luthier Ralph Novak, the man who developed the radical fanned fret fingerboard the guitar sported. I saw Hunter a few more times over the years and each time I came away even more impressed with his ability to transcend his own prodigious technique and just make music.

A few years after I first saw Hunter play I heard that he had the luthier Jeff Traugott build him an acoustic guitar. I had known Jeff from the beginning of his career and was excited to learn that one of the best guitarists I'd ever heard was working with one of my favorite luthiers. Not long after that I learned that Jeff was making an electric guitar for Hunter, the first one he ever built. The new Traugott guitar was a departure from the instruments that Novak built for Hunter. The most noticeable aspect was that it had seven strings instead of eight. The guitar still had three bass strings, but the guitar section was set up with four strings instead of five, the result of Hunter paring away any unnecessary elements that got in the way of the music.

Early in 2011, Jeff Traugott called and mentioned that Hunter was going to be playing in Santa Cruz, Traugott's hometown, and that he was going to be stopping by the workshop before the gig to have his guitar worked on. We both thought it would be interesting for all three of us to spend some time together talking about the process of ordering and building unique guitars. So I spent a good couple of hours in Traugott's shop talking with the luthier and the musician about the three guitars they had collaborated on in the past and the guitars they were going to work on together in the future.

FRETBOARD JOURNAL: Charlie, how did you hook up with Jeff? What were you looking for from him?
JEFF TRAUGOTT: I think the relationship actually started with me. I was a huge admirer of Charlie's for years and years. This is bit embarrassing, but I had a picture of him on my wall that I pinned a photo of a guitar that I made over the one he was playing in the hopes that someday he'd be playing one of mine. I went to his shows every time he came to Santa Cruz, but I never spoke with him because one of my friends, Ralph Novak, was building his guitars. Then it happened that Charlie was interested in getting an acoustic guitar and Ralph, who made mostly solid-bodies, actually hooked me up. The first guitar I made Charlie was an acoustic eight-string that he later sold.

This is the second iteration of the first electric guitar Traugott made for Hunter. Initially it had a scale length of 30" on the bass side and 25" on the treble side, but Hunter quickly discovered that it hurt his hands to play it. At first he thought the problem was caused by the guitar's deeper body, which made him hold the instrument differently than he was used to. Traugott then built a solid-body guitar based on the shape that Hunter and Ralph Novak developed, but with the long scale. It turned out that Hunter's hands still hurt, so Traugott made a new neck for this guitar with the scale lengths that Charlie was used to using, a scale length of 29" on the bass and 25.5" on the treble. The hand pain disappeared. The new scale length put the bridge in the wrong position, so Traugott had to make a new top so the bridge could set in the right place for proper intonation. Not long after getting the retopped guitar, Hunter realized that he never used the bridge pickup so he had Traugott remove it, which meant yet another new top. The original ebony string anchor on the back of the guitar was originally symmetrical, but its new shape shows how much the new scale length shifted the string position. "I could have made it symmetrical," Traugott says. "But that would have meant a new back." PAUL SCHRAUB PHOTOS

CHARLIE HUNTER: A guy in Japan has it now. Ralph sent me to Jeff because I wanted something that was more hollow and acoustic sounding. A couple of years after Jeff built that guitar for me I started playing seven strings instead of eight. Also, I found that even though it sounded great, it just didn't work for me on the road. I was always afraid of it getting crushed. So I went to Jeff to make a solid-body for me because Ralph was having some health problems and couldn't build.

FJ: Jeff, was it difficult making that first solid-body for Charlie? I don't think you'd made a solid-body before, let alone a seven-string with fanned frets and extra-heavy bass strings.

JT: I sure was figuring out all sorts of new things at the time, like what the tensions were on the bass and treble sides of the neck. Do I use carbon fiber neck reinforcements or not? Do I use mahogany or maple for the neck? Generally, mahogany's super stable as a neck material but maple is very dense. And Charlie, you require this pretty incredible curve on the bass side, but it's very flat on the treble side. It's a bit of a challenge.

CH: It is kind of a compound instrument and a compound concept, and so for the luthiers, it's definitely compound problems. There are problems Jeff has to solve that are not in the wheelhouse of standard guitar making.

JT: Take the truss rod, which is usually pretty simple. But on your guitar it has to adjust both sides of the neck in an equal fashion without losing that curve on the bass side.

FJ: Jeff, how many guitars have you built for Charlie altogether?

JT: There was the initial acoustic with eight strings that was sold to the guy in Japan. The second guitar was a semi-hollow body Model R, a body shape I developed, my most popular acoustic model. This guitar has gone through quite a few changes since it was first made.

FJ: Like what?

JT: I've replaced the top a few times. The first time to correct some scale length issues discussed below, which included a new neck, the second time making a change to the pick up configuration. The original version had three pickups, one for the bass

Charlie Hunter, on the right, holding the third iteration of the first electric guitar Traugott made for him, the version with the removed bridge pickup and pickup selector switch. Traugott is holding the koa solidbody he built for Hunter.

strings and two for the guitar strings. Charlie realized that he never used the bridge pickup so he had me remove it, which meant new top time. The back and sides are the only original parts left on this instrument. Speaking of the back and sides, I wanted to use Brazilian rosewood because I knew I could control the tone that way — the mids and highs. Then for the low-end I thought it would be really cool to get this kind of redwood sound going with the top, it has a really crisp, fat, high low-end, if that makes sense. So that's what I used on this guitar, and it's been quite successful from a tonal standpoint, the redwood's very soft, every ding shows, and I dinged it a couple times when I was working on it.

I have a strong feeling about tone. I'm unfamiliar with electric guitars. I realize that people talk about the swamp ash bodies, and certain ones that have a certain kind of tone, and there are spruce bodies, and there's all this different stuff. So, for me, I wanted to take this guitar and do a kind of ES-335 thing, but with a flat top. So, it's got a solid block down the center, but it isn't carved — it's not a super thick top. I wanted to emulate what I really like about my acoustic guitars, from a tonal standpoint, but I wanted to get — Charlie really likes the full range of tone, so I wanted to get that fatness in the mids and highs, but while still getting a really open low-end string. So that's why I chose Brazilian rosewood. It gives you that dark color. It's kind of like a cabernet wine, it's a really bold tone.

CH: I had Jeff make the semi-hollow body guitar with a longer scale length than my solid-body. Almost immediately when I began playing it I started getting pain in my hands.

JT: So instantly we thought, "Oh, it's the shape,"

because this is a different shape than his other guitars. It's also slightly deeper so we figured that had to be it. To try and remedy this I made Charlie the solid-body, my first ever, based somewhat on the design Charlie and Ralph had been using. He was still hurting, even with "his" body shape. Not long after that I got a call from Charlie saying, "Dude, I'm sorry, I need to have the original shorter scale length." I wasn't surprised to hear that as I never actually thought it was the best idea to change the scale lengths in the first place. Knowing how sensitive Charlie is to changes I figured this may cause more problems than it would fix. To make the solid-body comfortable again I made a new fingerboard with the tried and true scale lengths and fit it to the original maple neck. This guitar is really his workhorse, the all around go-to instrument.

FJ: So after the new fingerboard on the solid-body, how is it working for you now, Charlie?

CH: You can put a million miles on it and it will still be good. This one, you get in there and you're just like, "Wow, this is nice."

I'll tell you what, I've beat the living hell out of guitars. I play them every day, at least three hours a day, seven days a week and I'm on the road a lot. This thing, I don't baby the guitar, I play the hell out of it. I'm like the perfect canary in the coal-mine if you want to test your guitar out on the road. I mean, and you can just see, this guitar I've had for — what — two years now?

JT: Yeah.

CH: If you look at it, I've worn through the finish. And the intonation and playability are really good. You know, the fact of the matter is that any guitar is going to have intonation issues. I mean, there are certain areas on a Gibson guitar you try not to play on as

The photo of Charlie Hunter that Traugott doctored. The luthier hoped that one day Hunter would play a guitar he built.

The Hunter for Red Hot November: Charlie Hunter teams with drummer Scott Amendola on Monday night at Kuumbwa to prove that they are two of the grooviest jazz funksters around.

mentality about the instrument. Then eventually, I just came to the point where like, "Okay, I know what I need." Definitely, I know what I need. I know the window within which I need the guitar to operate. Then within that window, I'm totally happy to make adjustments. Because I'm good at making adjustments, because I've done this all my life, so I kind of know how to actually play the instrument.

JT: I think it might be good to talk a little bit about how in some ways it's not a guitar for you. It's actually a bass and a drum set.

CH: Yeah, I don't think of it as a guitar. I think of it as going away from the guitar, and I find that this allows me to take it even closer to the drum set. Not taking it closer to the drum set in a real obvious kind of analogous way, but in a much more kind of metaphorical way. I approach it like that in terms of, well, to me it's all covert chops, all the stuff that I do. I don't want to do anything that's going to impress most of the people in the world that would help me out financially. I'm going to do what I think is right for the music and for the instrument, and my concept, which is to play lots of counterpoint, and to push the music around contrapuntally from behind the scenes, rather than playing all of this stuff that's really up-front and obvious, and that everyone can do within a few months of playing guitar. That's why I feel like guitar, it can be a really incredible instrument for expression if you really spend the time on it, but it also can be a horrible device for hacking, and it is the number one hacking machine in the world.

But having said that, I would much rather listen to someone who's 14 years old just learning their first song in the first position, than listen to some people who you can click on YouTube and they're like the number one guitar thing on YouTube. I'd rather listen to someone just strumming a guitar, that's more exciting for me, because there's potential in that, you know.

FJ: Why did you choose a fanned fret instrument?

CH: I was doing this concept of a guitar that had a lot of range in it — really a bass and guitar in one instrument — and without the fanned frets I don't think I would really be able to do it. It wouldn't sound that good, you know. The only other option I could imagine would be like two entirely separate scale

much, and the same with a Fender.

JT: But you're uncompromising as regards to the playability and the action, and that kind of stuff — the intonation… and that has proven to be a little more challenging than I actually thought, just because trying to figure out what you need to do to these necks to make them work in conjunction with the body so it stays stable and travels well.

CH: After years and years and years of playing, you develop stuff, you get technique. At first, you definitely are going to go through a period of a kind of arms race mentality, and develop an obsessive-compulsive

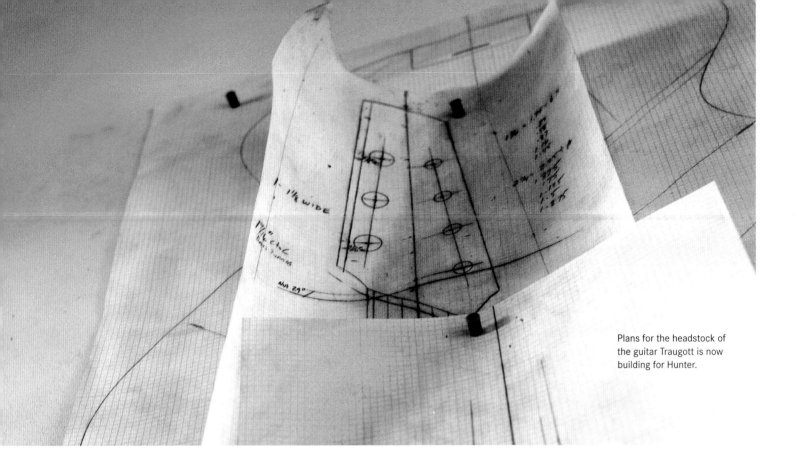

Plans for the headstock of the guitar Traugott is now building for Hunter.

lengths on the same instrument, which is a not a hard thing. I could totally easily play that; it wouldn't be a hard thing to play. To get back to the question, if I smashed everything into one scale, it just wouldn't sound good. The bass strings wouldn't have enough tension and would sound floppy, and the guitar section would sound kind of banjo-y.

JT: But when you decided to do this you knew Ralph already, and that's what kind of enabled you to get to the fan fret thing? Or did you know of the fan fret stuff before?

CH: I knew him already. I was playing a guitar that was just a regular 7-string. I was like, "Man, what about adding real bass strings to a guitar," and he says, "Oh, try this system." And I was like, "Oh, that's a good thing," you know.

JT: So the idea was to be able to have longer strings and shorter strings work in conjunction with each other and be easy to play.

CH: That's it. I mean, other stringed instruments are like that. Look at the piano and the harp. The bass strings are longer than the trebles.

JT: Yes, exactly. But why'd you start to play the mix of

bass and guitar? Because you were a monster 6-string guitar player, did you decide everyone's doing that?

CH: No, I just wanted more range and a little more just real tone, you know what I mean? Because the tone just wasn't that great with everything shoved into one scale.

JT: That's true. The low string is not as dynamic as it can be.

CH: No, it's not punching. It just disappears, you know, it just gets flubby. It gets real flubby.

FJ: Jeff, is it difficult to build a guitar with the fan frets?

JT: Yes and no. Cutting the fret slots has been a challenge for me, just because the layout has to be really perfect, and then I cut them by hand on this jig that I made using a chop-box-style kind of radial arm saw that changes angles. Charlie and I have been working on a fourth guitar that will incorporate all the lessons we learned with the first three. On that one, I will be using a CNC machine to cut the fret slots. With the computerized milling stuff, I'm able to give the information to a computer and then the operator can write a program to place the frets exactly where we want them, exactly. Then that information goes to a computer connected to a milling machine, and the mill then cuts the slots for us. That takes all the guesswork out of it. Ken Parker, who is friends with both of us, says that your frets can't really be out more than ten-thousandth of an inch, otherwise your guitar doesn't play in tune.

What's critical about fan fret instruments are that the string line is where the scale length lies. So figuring out where the string line is on the low string and the high string, and then laying out the frets underneath that string line exactly — laying out the scale lengths for the low scale — 29-inch scale length on the low string, and the 25 inches on the high string — getting that laid out perfectly, mathematically, right on the string line is pretty critical. So that's one of the interesting differences, though the frets appear to go to a vanishing point and, perhaps, from a mathematical standpoint they do, you can't just lay it out that way, you have to actually lay out the particular scale length underneath the exact string line for each of the high and low strings, and then use the common fret, in Charlie's case, #7, to connect those two strings perpendicular to the center line. Then use your compensation factor at the bridge, and then the guitar plays in tune.

CH: It's really, really important to me that my guitar plays in tune. I've got good relative pitch, and it comes from rhythm, because it's all about rhythm, and listening to rhythms. I want a third to sound a certain way, I want a fifth to sound a certain way. You have to hear how they beat together. I spend all my time playing with drum machines to work on my time and everything, but when you come to an instrument, you definitely have to realize that it takes a while to learn how to play specific instruments really in tune.

FJ: Are there guys out there trying to emulate your style now? Are people sort of following behind you saying, "I want a guitar like this?"

CH: Yeah, there are. I mean, it's a trip that there are, because this is a real time-consuming kind of pursuit. You really have to learn drums, and you really have to learn bass, and you really have to learn guitar. Then you really have to learn how to put all those things together.

But I feel like in the last 20 years I've done all the technical groundwork for it, and the people who do want to learn it, it's not — they can just go on YouTube and watch some videos, and learn how to do this stuff. I mean, you need to have the musicality, and you need to have the drive; not everyone is going to do it. But I know about 30 or 40 people who are doing it, and there are even a couple women in that group, which is kind of cool, you know. They're trying.

The two women I know who do it, it's really kind of hard for them, because they have real small hands. So they have to figure out different ways of doing it. It's not easy. It's just a lot of work and people don't really want to do it because it's so defined by this one guy, you know — me. I think when people are done they just think, "Well, so if I do that then at the end of the day I'm just going to sound like that guy. I don't know if that's really a great use of all of my time." But there are some people who are doing it, and some of them sound pretty damn good, actually, you know.

FJ: So, would you two work together again?

JT: Oh, yeah. It can be exasperating, though. I'll get a phone call from Charlie and he'll say, "Oh my God, it's so out of tune"! The action's insanely high!" Then I say, "Okay, buy this exact ruler, put this ruler up to the string, give me that exact measurement. And

Top: As you might expect, getting pickups for a seven-string guitar/bass hybrid can be a bit of a chore. Traugott and Hunter decided to get their pickups custom-made by Jason Lollar. The Lollars are taller than standard pickups, which allows for extra windings that give Hunter the specific tone he is looking for.

Middle: Traugott had to enlarge the string anchor on the back of the first electric guitar he built for Hunter to accommodate the new scale length when he shortened the neck.

Bottom: The back of Hunter's new guitar sports some lovely Brazilian rosewood. Unlike his other guitars, this one will be a non-cutaway.

don't lie." You get the measurement and you're like, "Okay, it only moved like a 1/64", it's not crazily out of adjustment."

But, to the musician — to you — any small changes, weather changes, or maybe how you feel physically, can mean that the thing doesn't play well, that day. But it is so cool, so inspiring to hear a great player performing on a guitar that I built. It sounds kind of corny, but it really is an honor and privilege to be part of that. So I learned a ton, and Charlie, it's great, because we do experiment a lot. I've had failures, I learn from those and get another chance to make improvements, in many ways that's what keeps me excited.

CH: Yeah, and I've had failures in what I've told him to do as well. So it's been a process, but it's constantly chipping away at all of the stuff to not do, and getting more and more of this stuff to do that makes more sense, and ultimately makes it more playable. And I've actually ordered another couple of guitars from Jeff. The next guitar he's working on, I think, is going to be probably like the Grail. It'll probably be the perfect mixture of these two guitars, the solid-body and the semi-hollow body, and all of the knowledge we learned in the experiments. The next guitar will be distilled, simplified. There's no cutaway, no bells and whistles in terms of construction. Everything — the scale length, the pickups, the bridge — everything on it is tried and true. So there's nothing to get in the way of the music. 🎸

Classically

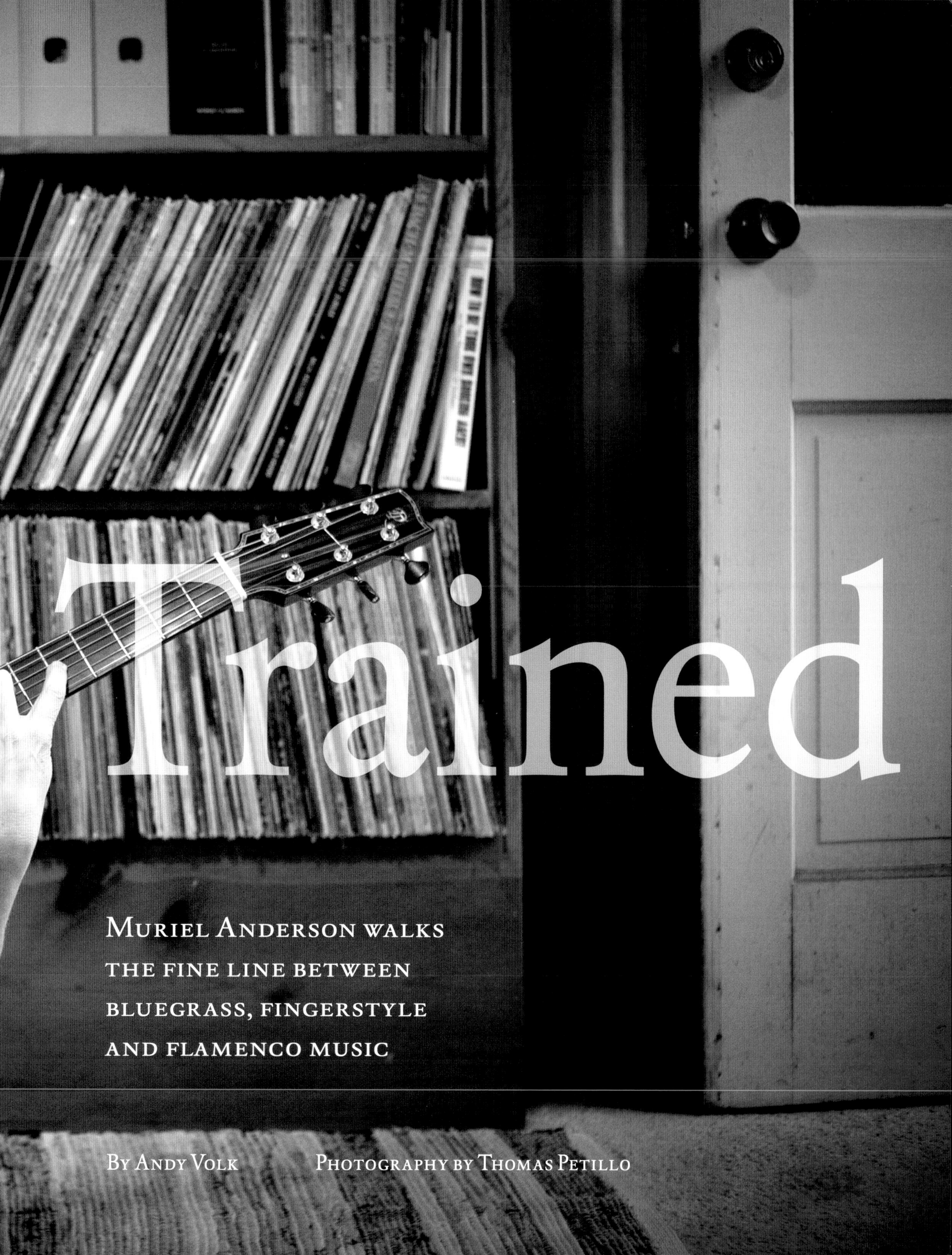

Trained

MURIEL ANDERSON WALKS
THE FINE LINE BETWEEN
BLUEGRASS, FINGERSTYLE
AND FLAMENCO MUSIC

BY ANDY VOLK   PHOTOGRAPHY BY THOMAS PETILLO

Anderson playing one of a pair of nylon-string Mike Doolin harp guitars. This guitar has an extra treble harp section positioned below the soundhole, while her other Doolin has a smaller body that was based on a requinto.

S OMEHOW, MURIEL ANDERSON, the petite woman cradling the nylon-string acoustic guitar on stage, morphs into an entire bluegrass band before our eyes and ears. It started with a credible imitation of clawhammer banjo on the classic fiddle tune "Old Joe Clark." "That leaves my thumb free so I'm going to play the bass line now," she says, describing her transformation into a one-woman banjo and bass duet in the matter of fact tone most people use to describe performing a mundane act like tying a shoe. This is pretty cool all by itself, but it gets better. "The index finger is the mandolin," she says. Now, the duet on grows into a trio and "Old Joe Clark" blossoms into "Foggy Mountain Breakdown," while the audience erupts in laughter and applause, thrilled to have witnessed this astonishing feat of musical legerdemain. Then, as Anderson follows the bluegrass barnburner with an exquisitely delicate raindrops-on-flower-petals rendition of the Japanese folk melody "Sakura," our shoulders sag in relaxed contemplation. Anderson is nothing if not versatile.

The first woman to win the National Fingerstyle Guitar Championship, Muriel Anderson is one of the world's most in-demand players and teachers on the acoustic scene. With a dizzying schedule of composing, master classes and international touring, as well as a producing a growing library of instructional books and DVDs, she's amazed audiences for 20 years with her technical command of the instrument while charming them with the subtle beauty, bubbling humor and warmth of her music.

"My parents got me a Doc Watson record for Christmas — it was *Good Deal! Doc Watson in Nashville* — and once I put it on the turntable it just never left."

I VISITED ANDERSON IN NASHVILLE to talk to her about how she got so dang good on the guitar. Like every great musician, it seems she started young. She wrote her first song while she was still in kindergarten, a song that was inspired by hearing the doorbell ring. She remembers running to the piano, finding the notes, harmonizing them and then adding lyrics.

Anderson came by her musical precociousness naturally. Her musical genes come from her mother, who taught piano at home, and her grandfather, Andrew Jacobson, who played alto saxophone in John Phillip Sousa's band. "My grandfather was the youngest member of Sousa's band at the time," she recalls. "I didn't know him very well because he died when I was young, but he was an inspiration because I thought playing music for a living was the coolest thing anyone could do."

Anderson started guitar lessons in grade school with Anne Jones at the Jones School of Folk Music in Lombard, Illinois, joining a children's bluegrass ensemble as she progressed on the instrument. "My parents got me a Doc Watson record for Christmas — it was *Good Deal! Doc Watson in Nashville* — and once I put it on the turntable it just never left. I played it over and over again and used to run home from school and try to figure out what he was doing. I learned

every song on that record." Anderson also picked up pointers from some more unusual sources. "When I got my first guitar I remember going outside and listening to the crickets, trying to imitate their sound on the strings and play along with them."

After graduating from high school, Anderson enrolled as a classical guitar major at Illinois' DePaul University, but hedged her bets at first with an apprenticeship in piano tuning in case the business of playing music didn't pan out. "I remember I was driving to college and I decided that at that moment, I was a guitarist," she says. "I was no longer a guitar student. My mother had taught me how to live off of rice and beans and I didn't need all those frivolous things like a house and a car that's all one color. I decided I was going to do whatever it took to be a guitarist, so I quit my piano tuning apprenticeship and put everything into the guitar."

At DePaul, Anderson studied with Leon Borkowski, a former student of renowned classical guitarist, Christopher Parkening. "I always just loved the sound of Parkening's guitar and his expression," she says. "I learned a lot of Parkening's really beautiful arrangements like 'Sheep May Safely Graze,'" she recalls. Borkowski wasn't a "touchy-feely" teacher. At one of her first lessons, he told her, "You have a terrible tone. Come back when you can get a better tone and

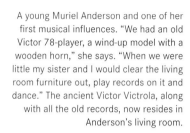

A young Muriel Anderson and one of her first musical influences. "We had an old Victor 78-player, a wind-up model with a wooden horn," she says. "When we were little my sister and I would clear the living room furniture out, play records on it and dance." The ancient Victor Victrola, along with all the old records, now resides in Anderson's living room.

don't come back before that!" Anderson says this tough love approach was exactly what she needed to hear at the time. She spent a week woodshedding every possible permutation on playing one note until she found her personal sound. "That was the most productive week of practicing I had in my life," she says. "It was a great approach for me, him challenging me and letting me discover a lot of the techniques on my own."

In her senior year at DePaul, Anderson was majoring in classical guitar but moonlighting in jazz and bluegrass bands. Though she enjoyed the challenges of changing genres on a daily basis, it eventually became tiring. She decided she would concentrate only on music with which she made a personal connection, regardless of genre. "I started playing just the music that made me happy," she explains, "Even though everyone told me I couldn't make a living doing that."

Anderson played local concerts, hotel lobby gigs, wherever people would be willing to hire an unknown instrumentalist who didn't sing. Not singing did lead to some billing problems. "Whenever I was listed in the paper as performing someplace, they would inevitably put 'singer-songwriter.' Because there was a picture of a girl with a guitar it was automatically assumed I was a

singer-songwriter." Anderson needed some kind of hook to let people know she played guitar but she didn't sing so she entered the National Fingerstyle Guitar Championship in Winfield, Kansas, in hopes of gaining some recognition to help promote her career. "I needed some sort of a title to say that I was a guitarist — not just someone who strums. So Winfield actually solved that problem. I was actually quite surprised and honored to have won."

The harp section on the Doolin harp guitar is set up with sharping levers that allow Anderson to raise the pitch a half step. This setup lets Anderson quickly tune the harp strings to any one of eight keys.

WHILE WALKING AROUND a nearby lake, I ask Anderson how she composes such stunning, orchestral arrangements. "I generally start with a tune or with a feel and then just see what it needs," she says. "The hardest thing is not what to add but how to make it as simple as possible and still get across everything that song wants to get across."

But what about multi-layered, polyphonic stuff like her finger-busting bluegrass medley? "When I first started working out that arrangement, I was just about at the point where I was ready to give up and say it couldn't be done," she replies, "Then I started to get it right for two or three notes in a row, then four notes in a row and then it all started to fall into place. It was a new technique I was developing with my

right hand in order to do that so it took a little while to feel comfortable. It seems sometimes it's just not working and then somehow, by the end, it's like riding a bicycle."

Ever attuned to her environment, Anderson stops our guitar-centric conversation in its tracks to appreciate the beauty of a herd of deer gliding past. She comes here often to appreciate the natural beauty of the state park and find inspiration in nature for her life and music. My inner guitar geek tells me this is a good time to change gears and talk about her guitars. I ask her about her first instrument.

"My first guitar was a half-sized classical guitar that I've since loaned to any number of nieces and nephews to learn on," she says. "My first good guitar was a steel string Guild. At the Newport Guitar

LESSONS FROM JETHRO, CHET AND LES

Having just one famous musician offer you sage advice, de facto music lessons and turbo boost to your career is a lofty goal for anyone. In Anderson's case, three legendary players contributed to raising her career profile.

As a college student at De Paul University, Anderson decided to take lessons with mandolin legend Jethro Burns, who taught in nearby Evanston, Illinois. "I went to mandolin lessons with Jethro more for humor lessons than anything else," she recalls. "He was so funny." Anderson's mother had often played "Nola," a finger-busting novelty ragtime piano piece composed in 1915 by Felix Arndt. After hearing Anderson's virtuoso guitar arrangement of the tune, Burns introduced her to his brother-in-law, Chet Atkins. Chet started sending cassette tapes of tunes for her to learn for her hotel gigs and Anderson responded in kind with tapes of her latest compositions. She began to visit Nashville, stopping by Chet's office for an impromptu lesson whenever possible. Anderson recorded Chet's composition "To B or Not to B" before he died.

"Chet was very unassuming," she remembers. "It was like talking to your uncle. He always had a foot firmly planted on the ground on which he grew up. He had friends ranging from the man who sold t-shirts out of the back of his truck to former presidents and treated them all the same. He always treated other musicians with a lot of respect and was always complimenting other musicians. He was always looking to learn new things, especially from younger players."

Les Paul came into Muriel's life in an equally unexpected manner. "I was playing a live late night radio show in Chicago on WGN — the Steve & Johnnie show. It was about one o'clock in the morning and they said, "There's a caller on line one. It's Les Paul." I said, "Okay, who is it really — you're pulling my leg." He came on the radio and said, "I really like your playing and if you're ever in New York on a Monday night come and sit in and play with me." So I did, a half a dozen times, at least. Les was always there with a joke. Always keeping you laughing."

"Contrary to expectations, Anderson found playing with these renowned musicians to be a pressure-less situation. "You knew that they were there to support you and I could feel that support as I played so it wasn't intimidating. It was joyful. If you look at my photos from the road with Les on my website you can see that we're both laughing in every photo."

Festival in Miami, a couple years ago, I walked to the end of the hallway to a display of historic instruments owned by the founder of the festival and there was an old parlor guitar that I bought from my first guitar teacher. It had been sold and re-sold. I picked it up, played it once and put it back in the display."

At the same guitar show, Anderson experienced that moment of guitar karma every musician hopes for, where you find a special instrument that seems to speak directly to your musical soul. "I was on my way to talk about getting a Flamenco guitar from Paris Banchetti when I walked past this David Taylor steel string parlor guitar and thought, 'That's the most beautiful inlay I've ever seen on a guitar,'" she remembers. "I picked it up and a sweet kindness just came out of this guitar. My breath was taken away. I thought, 'That's the sound I've been searching for my whole life!' I told him to put a 'sold' sign on it. I didn't even bargain," she says with a laugh. In a goose bump-inducing coda to the story, Anderson learned that Taylor had attended one of her guitar workshops, gone right home to his workbench and drawn up the designs for this very guitar. He'd chosen the inlay image of a wild rose he'd noticed growing in his backyard because he thought it described Anderson's personality.

Along with taking the six-string to new musical places, Anderson has been one of the most visible players in reviving the harp guitar, a turn of the 19th century instrument that adds additional bass strings to the guitar's standard voice. Anderson's interest in harp guitars began back at DePaul when she was playing Bach's cello suites. "They were just crying out for low, ringing bass notes," she says. "I had seen pictures of harp guitars and thought, 'That's what it needs.' Shortly thereafter, I went to a Michael Hedges concert because I'd heard that he played a harp guitar. I sat next to an older couple and it turned out they were writing a book on Larson guitars. [The Larson Brothers built the harp guitar Michael Hedges played that night.] They asked me if I would record the music for the book and I had the chance to play my first harp guitar."

Inspired by that recording experience, Anderson began a search for a harp guitar of her own. "Del Langejans built me my first harp guitar, a beautiful steel-string with rosewood back and sides and a cedar top," she says. "I also have a new 21-string nylon harp guitar made by Mike Doolin. I tune the bass strings in a scale going down from the sixth string. I'll vary that depending on what's needed in a specific song. Half-step tuners are handy for that."

Like every guitar geek, Muriel Anderson has strong preferences about the wood her guitars are made of. "For classical, Brazilian rosewood back and sides with cedar top has typically been my favorite sound," she says. "Now that I'm doing more flamenco-inspired music, I'm enjoying spruce tops and cypress or other lighter wood for the back and sides. For steel string guitars, I prefer spruce tops."

On the road as well as on many of her recordings, Anderson turns to her Morris signature model steel string. "I have to confess to quite a bit of Guitar Acquisition Syndrome these days," she adds. "I just ordered a flamenco guitar in spruce and cypress from Paris Banchetti. And I have two new guitars on order from my new favorite builder, David Taylor: a small steel-string harp guitar that I can bring on the road and another parlor guitar just like the one I have. I'd also love to have Linda Manzer build me a guitar some time."

Unlike some musicians who grow weary on the road, Anderson draws energy from travel and the possibilities it offers. "I take the time to enjoy my surroundings," she tells me. "Whenever possible, if there's some beautiful place to visit, I'll take the time to do so — as I'm doing right now. I also really enjoy meeting people. I stay with families much more than I stay in hotels. I'm a bit of a gourmet. I like to experience the cuisine of the area and appreciate really good food in general. There's even a whole section on my website, 'Recipes from the Road.' I really enjoy getting to know the people and I try to learn a little bit of the language each place I go. I've really been enjoying learning German lately. Tomorrow, I'm trading a guitar lesson for a German lesson."

Anderson's thumbnail has entered guitar lore. A few years ago she was playing at the Chet Atkins Appreciation Society Convention when fellow guitarist Jean-Felix Lelanne broke a fingernail. "So I cut off my thumbnail, glued it on to his fingernail, and he played the concert with it," she says. "We've recorded two CDs together since. We feel so much the same; we phrase the same way so it's like playing with my identical twin."

Recently, Muriel has been putting those German lessons to good use playing flamenco music with German musicians Raughi Ebert and Leo Henrichs, who perform as Tierra Negra. "I met them at a guitar festival in Germany," she explains. "Before long we started jamming and played late into the night. We started realizing that there was something really special happening. They're brilliant in knowing how to create the greatest feel without adding too much. It's been a wonderful experience to work with musicians who really understand when to be minimal and when to break out. Since we started playing music together, I've had a lot more music come out in my dreams; it just opened up the floodgates to new tunes."

Anderson reunited with the duo to record *New World Flamenco*, a collaborative CD of original music. "Each of us wrote a third of the material. There's their Nuevo Flamenco sound and I'm playing my harp guitar on some pieces. It turned out to be a beautiful combination. The slow, beautiful pieces really stand out in the context of the joyous Spanish-sounding pieces. When I first heard Tommy Emmanuel's music a light bulb went off: 'Ah! That's the joy of music.' The same thing happened when I met Tierra Negra."

In Anderson's view, it's this spirit of continuous inspiration and reawakening that helps her keeps that joy of making music alive. At this point in our conversation, our trip around the lake has come full circle, an apt metaphor for a musician whose entire career has been painted with curved brushstrokes; inclusive of the past but looking forward, too. "I've chosen the long road in a lot of ways," she says with a chuckle. "I feel compelled to share my knowledge and what I've been able to pick up to make it a shorter road for other people. I believe that sharing knowledge is an integral part of giving back as a musician." 𝕘

EASY
BEING
GREEN

The recycling artistry of motocross-racing, wood-logging, knife-building, fly-fishing luthier Larry Pogreba

BY DOC SIMPSON
PHOTOGRAPHY BY LYNN DONALDSON

"I made the headstock overlay on this guitar out of a beaver tail," Pogreba says. "We had a few beavers moving in and eating up all of our trees. There's no convincing a beaver to go someplace else once they decide to move in, but we made sure that we used every part of them that we could."

Opening spread: Larry Pogreba taking a break on Willow Creek. The motorcycle on the roof of the shed is a Yamaha 650 with a sidecar. "We won the sidecar motocross Nationals on that in 1976 and 1978," Pogreba says. "I retired from racing in 1979 when I hurt my back."

I **TURN MY CAR** down a gravel road just outside of Willow Creek, Montana, and cross miles of beautiful rolling hills and farmland. Soon, I pass a homemade black powder cannon with Cadillac Eldorado hubcaps sitting silently on a hill.

I'm getting close.

Further down the road, I see the wreckage of a small plane — its nose buried into the terrain, tail and wings shooting out of the ground in a spectacular fashion.

Almost there.

I pass over a cattle guard with plastic dinosaurs sitting atop two gateposts, and the dirt road narrows to a single winding lane. When I drive by an ancient abandoned barn and come around a hill, I am greeted by a 1970s motocross bike mounted on top of a small building.

This must be the place.

Welcome to the fantastic, eco-friendly imaginarium of Larry Pogreba. Pogreba and his wife, Donna, meet me with a warm greeting and invite me inside their home. Built from salvaged materials, it brims with whimsical touches. The walls of the main room are decorated with brightly colored South American art. Sawed-open guitar bodies are stacked with CDs. Light sconces made out of old hubcaps give off a soft glow. In the back of the room is an open kitchen; above the stove is the hood of a Studebaker, with working fan and lights.

The Pogrebas have been living in ecological harmony with the earth since long before going green became cool. They built their homestead completely off the grid, and the three buildings are constructed of recycled materials. Each one, including Larry's workshop, is powered by the sun and, only when absolutely necessary, a gasoline generator. The Pogrebas draw their water from a small stream that winds its way through the property. There are no electric wires or phone lines that connect them to the outside world. They don't own a computer, and they have to go stand on a hill to get cell-phone reception.

It is here, far removed from the blaring noise of a multitasking society, that Larry Pogreba quietly invents and creates. Some years back, after a local

and cultures. During second grade, his family was stationed in Georgia.

"There was a plantation right off the base," he recalls. "Me and my friends would sneak through the woods and listen to black gospel singing at night. I was just knocked out by that music. I had never heard anything like that."

About 1954, Pogreba discovered his first true musical hero. "We moved to our next base, in San Antonio. As we're driving across the country, I was

"WHEN ALL OF YOUR MOTOCROSS BUDDIES THINK YOU'RE CRAZY, YOU KNOW YOU'VE CROSSED THE LINE."

bowling alley went out of business, he set about building himself a cannon. "I managed to buy 400 bowling balls and 300 pairs of bowling shoes at a ganga price," he explains. He used the rear axle of a Cadillac Eldorado for the wheels, which explains the hubcaps. Today, in the wide, open spaces of Montana, Pogreba hosts cannonball parties; everyone sports bowling shoes, while he lobs bowling balls two miles into the distant hills. The cows are not amused, but everybody else is.

Pogreba (pronounced Po-gree-bah) drives a car he built himself from the parts of several discarded vehicles. He calls it the Pogrebamobile. It sports a chrome trout hood ornament and looks like a very hip British racecar. Even the startling plane wreck that greets visitors was recycled from a local airstrip; now, the surplus old aircraft makes for dramatic yard art.

In Larry Pogreba's hands, old stuff becomes new once more, which pretty much describes how he goes about building his highly prized hubcap resonators, Weissenborns, acoustics and electrics. It's been a weird, snaking journey, for sure.

Sneaking Through the Woods

Pogreba's father was a fighter pilot in the U.S. Air Force. That meant Larry and his two younger sisters grew up in a variety of countries

playing Ray Charles on the jukebox every chance I got. Dad was afraid we were going to get beat up."

During junior high, his father transferred to the Royal Air Force in England. "I went to English school — you know, with a little beanie hat and blazers." Then they moved to Germany for his high school years, where his interests blossomed. He began racing cars, studying martial arts and playing guitar.

"The first guitar I had was a Hofner archtop, " he remembers, "which my dad bought me. I didn't realize how hip it was until years later. He also bought me two records, Joe Pass and Django Reinhardt, which were completely over my head, since I was into old country blues and folksy stuff."

Tragedy struck in 1965, when his father was shot down over Vietnam. Rumored to be a POW, his father was never seen again. Larry Pogreba was 18.

He married right after high school. "That marriage didn't last very long, but I have a great daughter, Laurie." From marriage, he moved on to college. "In those days, there were no computers to keep track of people, so I would just take whatever classes I wanted to. I'd sign my [advisor's] and dean's names to my schedule. I went from taking writing to philosophy to fine arts. I mainly focused on fine arts." He learned to work with wood, metals, ceramics and resins — skills that would serve his creative inspirations for years to come.

In between classes, he cultivated his love of driving fast machines, and his specialty became sidecar motocross. "It was kind of the lunatic fringe that did sidecar motocross," Pogreba says. "When all of your motocross buddies think you're crazy, you know you've crossed the line." It became more than a hobby; he won Nationals twice.

Pogreba, it turns out, was also logging wood on the side. "The motocross racers would have jobs during different times of the year to support themselves. At the time, I'm living back and forth between Colorado and Kansas. I had a little place in Colorado, where we would cut firewood and then sell it in Boulder. Other parts of the year, my friends and I lived in Kansas. I had a little sawmill, so I would saw walnut, ash and oak. I built a wood splitter out of an old Cadillac. You could split three cords of wood an hour on it and still drive it around the yard."

His love of music grew, and he was starting to play a bit of guitar in local bars. "I actually got up the nerve to get in front of people and play folksy, bluesy stuff." As his guitar playing improved, he became more interested in the guitars themselves and how they functioned.

"In those days, there were no schools. The only book was the [Irving] Sloane book [*Classic Guitar Construction*], and that was on classical-guitar building. So I would just take an old guitar apart and put it back together. Then I got some wood and built a couple guitars. It was just kind of a hobby from the late 1960s until the mid-1970s, but when disco hit, I lost interest. Everyone was spending all of their money on polyester and cocaine. Acoustic music almost died."

Freight and Salvage

Pogreba continued his nomadic life until he met and married Donna, in 1976, and they settled in Colorado. With a new marriage came a new passion: building knives. "I had gotten interested in martial arts in high school. I was aware of the old Japanese tradition of making swords. I made my first laminated steel knife in 1976. In 1980, I heard there was a Japanese sword maker working for a knife shop there in Colorado." This was the legendary Japanese swordsmith Kuzan Oda.

"I went and met him; we hit it off and ended up sharing a shop together a few years later. He was very traditional Japanese. His family was, like, 600 years of samurai. When he was 12 years old, his family turned him over to a samurai master, who taught him how to make swords, jujitsu and all the standard samurai stuff. After his apprenticeship was over, the old master gave him a new name and kicked him out."

Now, Pogreba had a part-time logging business and pretty much a full-time job making knives. He would go to knife shows around the country and do fairly well. He also intensified his love for fly fishing, which he had been doing all his life. In the early '80s, he started going to Belize to do saltwater fly fishing.

"At that time," he notes, "they had a pretty backwards little country. Most villages had no electricity or running water; there was little by way of paved roads. Everybody drank beer and smoked pot. Now, they have cappuccino bars, internet cafes and hard drugs."

On one trip to Belize, an ocean storm forced them to make an emergency port, and they took some time to explore the surrounding jungle with their local guides. Pogreba noticed they kept walking past stumps where huge trees once stood. "The third one of these great, big stumps went by, and I asked, 'Is that mahogany?' They said, 'Oh, yeah,' so I cut into one of those stumps. It was good, sound wood. Next time, I took some big chainsaws down with me and I showed these guys how I wanted these stumps cut up."

These were mahogany trees that had been harvested a century before. "The stumps might be 12 feet tall, because they had been cut above the taper point. Sometimes, there were tops four feet in diameter. We got one tree that was left over from a forest fire. It was just a burnt-off snag, but was 45 feet tall, five to six feet in diameter and 10 feet into the ground. The wood was all cracked the first couple of inches, but after that, it was excellent wood.

"I built a lap electric for Darrell Scott out of that. I left some of the char marks and cracks showing on the back of the guitar where it didn't really matter. I just finished over them. There's the proof that it's salvaged wood."

The headstock overlay is made from rosewood burl. The hubcap coverplate come from a circa 1953 Mercury.

"I sometimes buy a large lot of hubcaps to get the three or four I need for guitars," Pogreba says. "These are a few of the hubcaps that don't work on guitars. I'm sure I'll find something fun to do with them one day."

His previous profession of logging firewood blossomed into a full-fledged South American enterprise. For the next 10 years, he coordinated with the locals to salvage wood from mahogany stumps and have it brought to the U.S. He also reclaimed exotic woods like granadillo, jobillo, nargusta, my lady, bullet tree, bastard rosewood, billy web, and "some things I had never heard of."

The venture was a financial success. "You can always turn good wood into money," he says, "but you can't always turn good money into wood." He salvaged wood from Belize until mahogany went on the endangered species list, in 2002.

big windstorm sometime in that 200 years can create 'ring checks' inside the tree. My experience has been instrument-quality wood is about one tree in 1,000."

Hubcap Heaven

Pogreba began experimenting with various woods, in part to find an alternative to rosewood. "The Belizean rosewood is very similar to Brazilian; I think it might even be better. The ingrain is denser, so I think it holds frets better. Some of the Honduras rosewood is pinkish — it's so light — but

"YOU CAN ALWAYS TURN GOOD WOOD INTO MONEY, BUT YOU CAN'T ALWAYS TURN GOOD MONEY INTO WOOD."

Meanwhile, back in the States, Pogreba was recovering from the disco disaster of the mid-'70s and started building guitars again in the early 1990s. "I always knew I would get back into building someday. One of the reasons I quit building guitars in the 1970s was because people were so stuck in tradition. If you were building acoustic guitars at that time, you were going to build Martins. Even Gibson copies were considered weird in those days.

"But in 1992, I saw Danny Ferrington's book on guitar building. Here he was, creating some pretty innovative stuff for most of my musical heroes. So that was when I realized that I'd probably get back into guitar building. The first half-dozen were flattops, just to get my chops back."

His 30 years of harvesting wood paid off. "That whole time, I was putting aside wood. When I was logging in Colorado, I would, on rare occasions, find a spruce tree that was good enough for guitar tops. They are not nearly as common as people might believe. Spruce trees tend to spiral while they grow, and then they are subject to all kinds of environmental damage. Anything big enough to be a guitar top is a couple hundred years old. Even a

the Belizean is not *Dalbergia stevensonii* [Honduras rosewood]. It's actually a slightly different wood than the Honduran stuff. It's darker, closer grained and has inky black streaks running through it."

Soon after he began building again, he started making resonator guitars. "I was putting a little popup camper in the roof of my Suburban. When I cut the sheet metal out of the roof, I had this nice, clean, flat piece of metal. I just cut it up and welded up a guitar body and made a nice resonator that weighed about 20 pounds. It actually didn't sound too bad. I built maybe two or three more out of sheet metal. But the sheet metal that was thin enough to produce a 10-pound guitar was a pain in the ass to weld.

"Then I realized I could make them out of aluminum. Aluminum is a third of the weight of steel. And you can get a much lighter guitar at 50 thousandths of an inch as compared to 30 thousandths of an inch with steel. Because of that extra thickness, you don't have the warping problem when you're welding it. Any cutting you need to do, you can just do it with a band saw. The soundholes I cut with a regular router. Any woodcutting tools handle aluminum just fine. So now I had this five-

MYSTIQUE

Jerry Douglas meets Larry Pogreba

I met Larry Pogreba after seeing his first guitars hanging on display at an early RockyGrass bluegrass festival back in the early '90s. While they piqued my interest, mostly because of their folk-art appearance, I didn't bite — even though I really wanted one. He uses real vintage hubcaps for cover plates on his resophonic-type guitars. Next thing I know, David Lindley is singing Larry's praises to me. I get more interested.

An old friend, the late, great Charles Sawtelle, was telling me about a buddy of his up in Montana who had built a cannon that used old bowling balls for ammo. Turns out it's Larry again.

Years later, I was leaving Merle Fest after a weekend of great music when Fender guitar A&R man Donnie Wade came up with this crazy, beautiful baritone-sized guitar that was a combo of National metal-body and Weissenborn. I had to have it. It sounded huge, and the 1954 Chevy hubcap and fingerboard covered with ancient coins, Smokey Bear and Elvis medallions beckoned to me. I've used it on records by Elvis Costello, Alison Krauss and Union Station, Sam Bush and others who never suspected it. All they knew was it sounded different than what they were expecting me to use and it was unique-sounding, adding a mystique needed in their song.

Larry invited me up to his ranch for a little cannon fire not long ago. He said the gophers were getting hip to his attack because of the whistling noise the bowling balls made with the three holes drilled into them. You can't win 'em all.

— Jerry Douglas

pound guitar, and you could anodize them these wild colors."

Pogreba's resourcefulness was only beginning. "People had always referred to resonators as hubcap guitars. The nickname was an inspiration. I thought, Why pay 40 bucks for a resonator cover that is exactly like everybody else's? So I started looking around and realized there were about a half-dozen hubcaps that were the right shape to be a resonator cover: the '54 Chevy, '54 Packard Clipper, '55 Olds, '62 Rambler, '55 Chrysler New Yorker and '53 Mercury."

In his quest for hubcaps, he would search out old garages along highways across the country. "One time, my wife and I were driving through Kansas. We drove into this place. It was a warm day. A guy walked out of a trailer — no shirt, barefoot. His big belly had pushed his pants down far enough that you could see about two inches of pubic hair. He had the same number of teeth and fingers. And then his son came out behind him, looked just like him. My wife said, 'I'm staying in the car.'

"Turned out, the guys had this great, organized pile of hubcaps. They had them separated by make and year in piles. They were two bucks apiece, cash. I was like, 'Wow, I'll take that pile and that pile…' They couldn't believe their good fortune, but I was able to buy a whole pile of '55 Olds hubcaps for two bucks apiece."

The hubcap resonators sounded good to Pogreba; he just had to figure out the neck angle. "The tension on a resonator is pretty critical," he explains. "You want to get a balance between fundamental tone and harmonics. The neck angle is a real subtle thing. You can tip it back very slightly to get more volume, but you might lose some of the harmonics and even the bass response."

Pogreba prefers koa for the biscuits and Belizean rosewood for the saddles on his resonator guitars. "I've tried a lot of different materials, and I always go back to that. I used to put screens over the ports in the body, and then at one point, I could see one of them was loose, so I poked it out while I was playing the guitar, and I immediately heard a better bass, so I quit putting screens in."

Further Exploration

Though perhaps best known for building resonators, Pogreba has done a lot of experimenting along the way, including a few 30-inch-scale archtop baritones. "I like the note separation you get with an archtop," he says, "as compared to what you get with a flattop. But a flattop is just a warmer-sounding guitar, so I would X-brace these archtops, but do a regular acoustic-style pin bridge. You get a big, warm baritone guitar that still has good note separation, and then you tune it down to an A, and that long scale gives you a chimy quality, almost like a piano. Darrell Scott has one of those."

He's also expanded into building Weissenborn-style acoustic lap-steels; he uses antique coins for fret markers and sometimes carves the bodies into whimsical shapes — including that of a woman's derrière.

"I have a baritone Weissenborn that is amazing," says David Lindley, who calls Pogreba one of his favorite builders. "Koa top and back and rosewood sides. It sounds like a big piano that can slide. I have one baritone that is two guitars in one: a baritone on one side, flip it over, and it's a regular-scale Weissenborn on the other. So it has two soundholes, and you can see right through the instrument. It sounds like a normal guitar, even with a soundhole in the back."

Pogreba has been building electric guitars for a while as well. When he first got back into the building business, he was, like a lot of acoustic-guitar builders, kind of an acoustic-guitar snob. "I didn't really have a very high opinion of electric guitars. But then I got interested in old tube amps, so I built a few electric guitars and plugged them into an old tube amp. And for me it was, 'Wow, I get it now.'"

When it comes to electrics, he notes, "I'm not trying to build the best Stratocaster. I do neck-through guitars with spruce bodies. They are lighter-weight guitars that are a lot more resonant, but because of that, you don't get the real clear, fast single notes that you want for playing leads. But they're great slide guitars. Plus, it only weighs four pounds;

you don't even know you're wearing it. It's not going to be everybody's first choice, but it fills a niche. And that's all I need to do. I don't need to sell a hundred of anything. So if I can sell five electric guitars a year, that's as many as I want to make."

As with most of his creations, Pogreba takes an eco-friendly approach toward building guitars. His use of recycled materials gives a rough-hewn aesthetic to his creations. He re-uses strap pins, and pickups come from beat-up, old flea-market guitars. He also incorporates horns, bones, shells and teeth that he picks up off the ground. When he was still building knives, he made several pieces out of meteorites. He saved up the excess shavings and later melted the metal into slide bars for his resonators. Once, he bought an old kitchen table at a yard sale and got 20 necks out of it. Pogreba admits that it would be cheaper for him to buy his parts new from a supply shop, but taking something old and giving it new life is clearly his passion.

There is no question that Pogreba's creations reflect superior quality and original craftsmanship, but he makes no effort to hide the welding seams or the hammer marks created when pounding a back arch into shape. "Everything I build shows speed. Most custom-guitar builders today get 10 grand for a guitar. I still sell electrics for a thousand dollars and resonators for two thousand." Each Pogreba guitar requires roughly 30 to 50 hours to build. "Like I said, my stuff shows speed; a good-sounding, good-playing instrument with a serviceable finish."

Pogreba's recycling bug has led him to restoring old tube amps. "Back in the early 1990s, you could buy a tweed [Fender] Deluxe for 300, 400 bucks. Obscure tube amps were going for $100." A guy just outside of St. Louis wanted one of Pogreba's resonator guitars, and he traded about 14 old tube amps for it. "They were weird, off-brand stuff. About half of them were really good. And that's what got me interested. Then, the vintage thing started to kick in. All of a sudden, a tweed Deluxe went from $300 to $700 to $1,000. And I was thinking, That's a lot of money for that old amp. Now, they're $3,000, $4,000.

"Leo Fender was building out of the same RCA

tubing that everybody else was building out of. So you could buy these old tube PAs at second-hand stores for $5, then bring them home and realize it had the same circuit as a tweed Pro. So, you can sell your tweed Pro and keep your $10 amp that sounds just like it. I started farting around with those — the PAs and the more obscure amps."

Pogreba points to a shelf packed with old amps. "Like that little Oahu up there: You could buy that amp and the lap-steel it came with for $100. Now, that amp would probably bring around $800. That's just crazy."

Discovery

The first guitar hero Pogreba sold an instrument to was Johnny Long, a Denver-based blues guy; the first internationally known was Keb' Mo'.

"I was driving through Boulder and I heard he was going to be on the radio," Pogreba recalls. "I had one of my guitars in a music store, [Robb's Music]. I went by, grabbed the guitar and went to the radio station. I walked in just as he was walking out. He sat down and played it, liked it and said, 'My wife's going to shoot me if I bring home another guitar.' So I said, 'Well, you can trade me for her gun.'"

Not long after that, Bonnie Raitt played on an album with Keb' Mo, and during the sessions, she was admiring his newly purchased Pogreba resonator. "I heard through the grapevine that she was interested in one," Pogreba says, "so I talked with people who knew her and just went ahead and built one for her. I found out what her preferred neck shape was, what gauge strings she played, her favorite color. While I was setting things up, I was listening to her records, just to help get the right vibe. So I built a guitar as near as possible to what I thought she would like. It was a smaller body, kind of a purplish blue. I used a '62 Rambler hubcap, 'cause that's got a big 'R' on the front."

To accommodate the height of the hubcap, Pogreba cut a circle in the top of the guitar's hard-shell case and covered it with another hubcap. He gave the neck a bit more of an angle, because he knew she plays .011 to .050 strings, then anodized it blue and gave it a "quick dip in the purple pot."

"This blue guitar was painted by a friend of mine who paints Harleys for a living," Pogreba says. "I found the pickup at a garage sale on a homemade guitar made out of a two by four. It's really microphonic — you can actually sing through it — but it sounds great."

"This hubcap is from a 1956 Chevy," Pogreba says, "This finish is the result of an anodizing experiment that didn't work so I added some paint to make it look I meant to do it that way."

"I sent it to Bonnie," he says, "and she liked the guitar. She's not a guitar junkie; she doesn't have 30 guitars. I think she has her old Guild, that old brown Strat of hers and a couple of purple Fender Bonnie Raitt models and maybe a Gibson electric. But she doesn't have a lot of guitars like you might expect. She took it on the road and gigged with it for a week before she decided she wanted to buy another guitar.

"There are plenty of people who could give her a guitar; she could have hundreds. But she is not going to take advantage of somebody who wanted to give her a guitar. She bought that guitar. She just wanted to be sure that was what she wanted."

Eventually, Raitt ended up with three of Pogreba's guitars, and the word about his craftsmanship spread. Jackson Browne, Jerry Douglas, Martin Simpson and Sonny Landreth each got on board. Emmylou Harris plays a guitar that features a Nash Rambler hubcap — made, of course, in honor of her band, the Nash Ramblers. Darrell Scott has ended up with eight Pogrebas. As it happens, Pogreba had just showed Scott a couple of guitars a few days before my arrival.

"One that I liked the best was strung up with light strings," Pogreba explains. "The other one was a bigger, stiffer guitar with mediums; I thought it was a little more work to play. And that was the one that Darrell picked up and liked immediately. He is just a much more powerful player.

"You've built this guitar; you have it around for a couple of weeks; you're playing it, doing the setup — you think you know what it sounds like. Then you hand it to someone like Darrell Scott, and you're like, 'Oh, my God. It never made that sound for me!'"

David Lindley bought four for himself and got one for his daughter as well. Lindley was once trying out some different Pogrebas during a small bar gig when he picked up a particular beauty. "He said, 'Wow, look at the way this thing focuses.' And he was just aiming it at people around the room, and they would turn their heads when he aimed it at them. And I was like, 'How did he know that?'"

Future Stock

Reflecting on the road ahead, Pogreba suggests that he's ready for a change in direction.

INSPIRED WHIMSY

For Bonnie Raitt, it's hard to separate the man from his instruments

What I love about Larry's guitars are qualities that stem so much from his uniqueness as a person. He's thoroughly delightful to interact with, and his passion, originality, deep connection to the materials he uses — the absolute unique design and sound of each one — make his guitars truly original works of art. I have three that are each so different from my other guitars and very dear to me.

The most showcased publically is the purple cutaway "National" resonator guitar, fashioned from recycled aircraft aluminum, salvaged wood on the neck and fretboard and a '51 Nash Rambler hubcap with an "R" for my last name as the pie-plate cover. It has two pickups and controls that allow you to switch from an all-acoustic to electric sound or mix the two. I use equal parts of both and, on my last tour, played through my compressor and Bad Cat amp to help it cut through with the band. If I'm playing it alone, I just go through a DI [direct input].

It plays like a dream, sounds great and looks totally badass. It's like driving a custom hot rod, and I was delighted when he surprised me with it. Jackson [Browne] loved mine so much, I think he had Larry make him a similar one.

The other two guitars Larry made for me are beautiful as well. One is a very light electric made of bamboo and spruce; the other is a new parlor acoustic made of mahogany, koa and jobillo woods. Both are portable enough to be perfect bus and living room instruments to play for fun and writing. The electric sounds great on slide or regular-tuning songs, and the acoustic similarly has a sweet, sensual feel and warm, intimate sound. I can crank the electric up loud on the gig, and it sounds just as mighty and funky as I'd like as well.

I love that Larry is so conscious in picking and recycling the wood for his instruments. Like a great artisan and sculptor, he lets the materials tell him how they want to be shaped. There's as much inspired whimsy as there is deliberate craftsmanship in his guitars. And I love who he is, and where and how he chooses to live, as much as I do his instruments.

It's an honor and a delight to play his guitars.

— **Bonnie Raitt**

The coin inlays on the neck of this koa Weissenborn-style all date from the 1800s.

"I'm sort of tired of the metal-bodies," he says. "The guy who was welding them for me, he was tired of welding them. The guy who was thinning the resonators had a heart attack. The guys that were doing the anodizing were having some health problems. You know, with the resonators, it's just kind of over; I've built enough of them. I've got three, four more aluminum bodies that I'm going to get to some of my guitar heroes. I'm going to build mostly acoustic guitars. I'll still build a few electrics, because I like them. I'll build some wood resonator instruments."

And the inventive explorations for Pogreba will continue. "There's this archtop idea I have with fiber rods. I got carbon-fiber rods that are connecting the neck block with the tail block. This keeps the guitar from collapsing from string tension, but it also supports the string tension that pushes down on the top. Because of that, I would be able to carve the top very thin — with a top that worked like a speaker cone.

that luthiers of today are particularly well equipped for the job.

"We know more about guitar building, and the techniques are better," he explains. "In the 1930s, they had better material, but I think, in 20 years, we're going to look back and realize some of the best guitars ever built were being built today."

Living off the grid during Montana winters can get rough. There are weeks at a time when the Pogrebas can't get to civilization. To compensate, they've just finished constructing a home in New Mexico (out of recycled materials, naturally) where they will spend the colder months. Donna passes her time as a weaver, and Larry pursues sculpting and songwriting. But the inventor in him never tires. (He is currently working on creating a "low-head hydro unit" to create power from streams and is exploring ways to improve wind machines.)

One of the marks of true brilliance is the ability to see the extraordinary within the ordinary. Driven

"[KEB' MO'] SAID, 'MY WIFE'S GOING TO SHOOT ME IF I BRING HOME ANOTHER GUITAR.' SO I SAID, 'WELL, YOU CAN TRADE ME FOR HER GUN.'"

"The normal archtop is a quarter-inch thick under the bridge and maybe an eighth of an inch thick in the re-curve area, but this one is about an eight of an inch under the bridge and about a sixteenth at the re-curve. I'm going to try cutting it just a little thinner." His experiment seems to be working; the carbon fiber rods are doing their job. "The action hasn't changed at all, which tells me the top is still staying at the right height, so there may be some promise in that."

Pogreba doesn't indulge in glossy finishes or elaborate inlays; he just wants to, in his words, "provide a good tool." At 64, he seems intent on building fewer guitars — and on trying to play them a little more — but he won't quit building them, he stresses, because he loves doing it and he believes

by a unique vision and passion, Larry Pogreba takes common pieces of wood and metal and shapes them into uncommon instruments. Keep that in mind the next time you're driving in the backcountry of Montana, and you hear the whistle of a bowling ball flying high overhead or you see the tragic wreckage of a crumpled airplane. Don't worry: You've simply entered into the backyard of a green genius. 🎸

ON THE ROAD WITH
JACKSON BROWNE
AND DOZENS OF
VINTAGE GIBSONS

LOAD OUT

BY JOHN THOMAS
PHOTOGRAPHY BY PETER DIANTONI

"I'm so sorry," Jackson Browne whispers hoarsely. "I can't do the interview. It's been a crazy day. I'm quite sick and I almost cancelled the show. I still might."

It's about 4:00 PM and I've just arrived to interview Browne and watch the sold-out show at the Connecticut stop of his tour with long-time collaborator David Lindley. Browne is suffering from a nasty flu that appears to be heading rapidly toward walking pneumonia. This afternoon he managed to visit a physician and get some medication, but he looks exhausted and is clearly not up for an interview, let alone performing before 5,000 fans.

Jackson Browne and David Lindley soundcheck at Milwaukee's Riverside Theater on September 24, 2011. Browne is playing a Gibson FJN (Folk Jumbo Natural).

Jackson Browne soundchecking each and every acoustic guitar he'll play before a concert at Southam Hall at National Arts Center in Ottawa, Canada. Photo by Tom Laveuf. *Opposite page:* David Lindley on his Paddy Burgin-built Weissenborn.

But two things keep Browne from sending me packing. The first is that he's as gracious and generous a person as you'll ever meet. It pains him not to be able to fulfill his promise. The second is the guitar case in my hand. Knowing that he loves old Gibson guitars, I emailed him that I'd be bringing my 1943 Southerner Jumbo to show him during the interview. He's clearly intrigued by the case, and as he looks at it, his tired eyes show a bit of sparkle. Finally, his curiosity overcomes his illness and he says, "Well, why don't you come back for a few minutes before you go."

I follow Browne down a hallway, his flu-ridden body relegating him to more of a shuffle than a walk. We enter his dressing room. I open the case and hand Browne the guitar. Barely looking it over before picking a quick arpeggio, Browne looks up as the notes sustain and breaks into a wide grin. He spots the band's guitarist, Mark Goldenberg, walking by and croaks as loudly as he can, "Mark, you've got to hear this guitar." Browne hands the guitar to Goldenberg and then leaves the room. Goldenberg is playing some beautiful, jazz-tinged fingerpicking, when Browne pops back into the room with David Lindley in tow. "David, you need to play this," he says, and then he heads back out the door.

Moments later, Browne reappears with two well-loved guitars in hand. "These are my first two Smecks," he says as he hands one 1930s Gibson Roy Smeck Stage Deluxe to me while he sits down and cradles the other. He plays one for a bit, talks about what he hears and nods to me, "Now, play that one and listen to the difference. You know, I'm not a one-axe guy, I just can't be, and the differences that you hear between these two guitars that should be exactly alike explain why."

I'm mindful that Browne is tired and stand up to leave. But before I can say good bye, Browne looks over and says, "John, you need to play the other guitars." He lifts himself from his seat and leads me out of his dressing room and toward the stage and a rack of about 20 guitars. As he quickly says "try this one," "OK, now this one," or, "look at this," it becomes clear that this is the abbreviated tour of his stage arsenal. But, it is equally clear that he really meant "need." As tired as he is, as worried as he is about tonight's show, he honestly appears to want me to understand the musical value of each instrument. I have simply never met anyone so passionate about guitars, so attuned to an instrument's nuances, or so articulate about tone. In a few hours' time, I'll marvel at how the combination of professional commitment and modern pharmaceuticals will enable Browne to put on a riveting, nearly three-hour bravura performance. But right now, all I can think about is that my quest is over: I've found the fearless leader of the Guitar Geek Nation.

"If you took the covers off of those piezo boxes, grown men would weep when they saw how they were made."

Two weeks later, I meet Browne again. He's looking much better and is in the midst of a soundcheck at New York's Beacon Theater. The band is playing "Giving That Heaven Away," a tune from Browne's 2008 album, *Time the Conqueror*. While Goldenberg brings the tune to a close with a scorching solo, Browne's guitar tech runs from the wings with one of the new Gibson Jackson Browne Smeck prototypes. The concert is going to be filmed and Browne talks the director through each tune, telling him about the dynamics of verse and chorus, where a "big drum fill" or "great bass lick" occurs. He wants the filming and lighting to focus on the musician who should be in the spotlight at a given moment.

Browne and Lindley. Browne uses both Roy Smeck Stage Deluxes and the blonde Roy Smeck Radio Grande shown here.

But he's also careful to warn the director that music is not scripted. "You know, we play differently every time. You can't really film it now and then splice it in. We always play it how we feel like playing it."

Away go the cameras and out come even more guitars. The crew sets up for the opening acoustic set by Browne and Lindley. Five songs require five guitars. A 1946 Gibson LG-2, two 1940s Martin 00s, a modern Martin D-41 and a Gibson Roy Smeck Radio Grande reissue all get the Browne treatment. He plays each, talks with the sound engineer, plays some more and only puts a guitar away when satisfied with the mix for each.

Less than an hour later, Browne and Lindley take the stage for their opening, acoustic set. From the first note and throughout the three-hour show including the full-band electric set, all of the guitars sound great, each sounds different from the others, and each is matched to the tune on which it is played. Browne picks a melancholy song on a doleful sounding guitar tuned a step below concert pitch. For an upbeat tune, and, as Browne quips, "the thing about my happy material is that there's really not that much of it," he switches to a guitar with a bright tone. But like a good film director, Browne also knows when to cast against type. So, a gloomy arrangement might be treated to a luminous-sounding instrument for contrast.

Two categories of questions cross my mind as I watch the show. First, I wonder how Browne goes about matching an instrument's voice to a song. Which comes first, guitar or song? Does Browne ever decide that his initial evaluation is wrong and switch guitars? Does he ever change guitars for a given song depending on the mood he seeks to set on a particular night?

But, I've also got a more basic question: why? At concert's end, 3,000 ecstatic New Yorkers are standing, cheering, and dancing in the aisles. In a few moments, the throng will spill out onto the sidewalks of Broadway while laughing, still dancing and shouting to their friends that this is the best concert that they have ever attended. And, truth be told, likely not a one of them cares about the tone of a single guitar that Browne played.

On the last stop of Browne's tour in Milwaukee, I get to ask those questions. He has spoken eloquently on the topic throughout our afternoon-long chat. But, in truth, the answer is even clearer in his facial expression as he holds up a little 00-17 he bought for his goddaughter. When he connects with an instrument, he *really* connects with it. The joy that he gets simply from cradling this guitar and picking a few notes it is nearly palpable. Moreover, he clearly has a compatriot at his side in David Lindley. Browne picks up a nearly identical "but really different" 00-17, and says, "These things rule." Lindley nods in agreement.

As they work through sound check, each choosing a different instrument for every tune, they listen for the blend of dual instruments and dual singing voices. "That sounds *really* good," Lindley says as Browne silently communicates his assent by putting away the second 00-17 and taking a 1994 Gibson Roy Smeck Stage Deluxe reissue from the guitar rack.

The Smeck, Browne says, "was my main guitar for quite a while. But I haven't found another new one that sounds this good." He first noticed these unusual Gibsons in the hands of the likes of Ry Cooder, Jerry Jeff Walker and Norman Blake. "But, I just wasn't a Gibson guy back then and they didn't really register with me." That changed in 1990 or 1991 when Browne encountered a Stage Deluxe in a New York City guitar shop. "I picked up this Smeck and it just sounded so big and deep," he says. He bought it and dubbed it Number One. So taken was Browne with the tone of that guitar that he's since purchased an even dozen vintage Stage Deluxes. "I ended up giving a bunch of them away and some of the ones I gave away were really good. I don't know what I was thinking, except I was trying to get one as good as the first one. But, there's really nothing like the first one."

That search for a perfect guitar is an integral part of who Browne is. There are two facets to Browne's guitar absorption. His description of the first borders on the lyrical. "Guitars all have songs in them. The way you play a particular guitar winds up being a quality that the song has and can keep." Browne isn't so inflexible that he won't try a song on another guitar. "But," he adds, "when all is said and done, you imbued the song with the way you played it, on the guitar you wrote it on."

I ask Browne how he came to "understand" guitars. "I think that having a lot of guitars is partly a consequence of spending a lot of time with a guy like David Lindley who knows a lot about guitars, knows there are a lot of great guitars, and knows how different they all are, and how valuable they all are in a myriad of different ways."

There was a practical component, too. "I began playing in different tunings. First dropped D, then double dropped D or dropped G." His earliest guitar friends and mentors such as Steve Noonan played in different modal tunings and were always making up different tunings. Introduced to the wonders of alternate tunings but playing live and not having time to retune for every song, Browne immediately discovered the usefulness of a stage with multiple guitars.

"It took me forever to figure out that you don't want the same thing from every guitar," Browne says while quietly playing Number One. He really went off the deep end for Gibsons for a while, first for the Smecks and then for the LG-2s. "The LG-2s have that fat neck that I've become accustomed to," he explains. "They also have that comfortable, small body." For his album *Time the Conqueror*, he used an LG-2 both for the soft fingerpicking and for just "pounding on the thing," he says. "The great thing was that you could hear every bit of the guitar, in all parts of the arrangements."

Browne's thoughts turn to tonewoods and one of his first "good" guitars. "I had this [Martin] D-18 that didn't have what my friends said their D-28s had, so I had to get a D-28." He then turned his back on mahogany for a while. "I thought that mahogany was too bright, didn't have the bottom end. But, then Gibson made me those Smeck prototypes and I liked

"It took me forever to figure out that you don't want the same thing from every guitar."

In his never ending quest for tone, Browne has taken to modifying some of his favorite electrics, like this 1961 Gibson SG, which now boasts a Teisco Del Rey pickup in its neck position.

In the late '90s, Browne dropped some of his favorite vintage Smecks off at the workshop of luthier Roy McAlister. McAlister studied them extensively and built two Smeck-inspired guitars for the singer-songwriter.

the mahogany." In fact, for the backs and sides of the new production model, Browne chose the "middle ground" between mahogany and rosewood: walnut. "Now," he adds with a laugh, "I hear people saying that mahogany is a softer wood [than rosewood], so it has a mellow, warmer tone and I'm thinking, 'Have I had this wrong for 35 years?'" If he had it wrong, Browne's got it right now. He does play a rosewood Smeck reissue and a Martin D-41, but most of his other stage guitars — vintage Smecks, LG-2s, Gibson FJN, those 00-18s — are mahogany.

"Look," says Browne, "what I care most about is amplifying the thing." In front of us stands one of his huge touring cases that hold a dozen guitars in stand-up racks. The cases open and close like giant, rectangular metal clamshells, leaving the guitars in the stands. The guitars only make the cut and into the racks if they sound great acoustically and amplified. "There are a million guitars out there that sound great, but if you can't get it to sound good live, it ends up sitting around in your bedroom. I'm not interested in that at all." As if to emphasize the point, to our right, where David Lindley will be sitting an hour from now, is a circa 1940s metal sign bearing the mantra, "Louder Music is Better Music." The roadies put the sign there for comic effect next to a "master list" of song titles matched to instruments and tunings.

The first pickup system that really impressed Browne was the Flat Response Audio Pickup, or FRAP as it is now known. The system's inventor, mathematician Arnie Lazarus, began making the pickups in 1969 and by 1973 had built about 500 of them. Depending on the model, the pickup consisted of one to three piezo crystals housed in a tiny box that was attached to the underside of a guitar's top. Browne thought that the FRAP sounded good, but ultimately found them to be problematic. "The preamps, you had to keep them close to you because you lost quality with longer cables," he says. "And the boxes were all different because they were handmade." Even the successful installations did not always end happily, because the pickups were fragile and difficult to repair. "If you took the covers off of those piezo boxes, grown men would weep when they saw how they were made,"

says a now-amused Browne. "It just couldn't be fixed. There were parts that were potted so no one knew what they were. Every one of them looked different."

So, Browne went looking for an alternative and found it in the Trance Audio Lens System, which was developed by Gary Hull, who used to work for FRAP. "It's a sort of second-generation FRAP idea." Browne looks pensive for a moment and leans forward and says, "And, this is *the* most important thing: it doesn't change the sound of a guitar like any of the systems that have a piezo element running along the bottom of the bridge saddle. Not only do those only measure the sound that that little piece of bone gets, but they restrict the movement of the bridge and interfere with the contact between saddle and bridge. And, I can hear the difference. When you have a really great guitar and you put the Trance Audio system in, there it is, that guitar, only louder."

The tweaking is worth the effort. "Every guitar that has this system just sounds like itself." Browne has had the Trance Audio installed in "20 or 30 guitars." The installation, however, has not always been a success. "Some guitars," says Browne, "resist" the pickup. "I've got this one great McAlister that just doesn't sound good with the pickup. Roy's theory is that the X in the bracing is so wide that it doesn't provide a really contained, kind of pyramid-shaped area in front of the bridgeplate to focus the sound. But, it's a great guitar."

Jackson Browne's musical partnership with David Lindley began more than four decades ago when Browne was still in high school. Browne was a member of the Nitty Gritty Dirt Band, but had already made the decision to leave the group to follow his own songwriting muse. Attending California's Topanga Canyon Banjo Fiddle Contest, he encountered Lindley, who was serving as judge after having been disqualified from further competition because he had won the contest the past five years.

"There are a million guitars out there that sound great, but if you can't get it to sound good live, it ends up sitting around in your bedroom. I'm not interested in that at all."

Guitarist Mark Goldenberg plays an Archilaud built by luthier Flip Scipio.

The two began running in the same musical circles. Lindley was on hand when Browne played his first gig at L.A.'s famed Troubadour club, opening for Linda Ronstadt. Lindley sat in on fiddle when Browne played "These Days," and the musical chemistry was immediate. "It was like we had been playing together forever," says Browne.

In the years following the Troubadour gig, Browne attained stunning success as a songwriter, seeing his songs recorded by The Eagles, Linda Ronstadt, The Byrds, Tom Rush, and the Velvet Underground's Nico. When in 1971, Browne signed with Asylum Records to record his first album, it was only natural that he recruited Lindley to serve as lead

guitarist in the band. A decade of close collaboration and a string of dazzling albums followed, from 1973's *For Everyman* through *Late for the Sky*, *The Pretender*, *Running on Empty* and 1980's *Hold Out*. As a testament to how fans feel about the Browne/Lindley union, Lindley's very presence on the bandstand in the recent tour brought cheers and his lap steel solo on *Running on Empty* frequently provoked standing ovations.

The reunion of Browne and Lindley has occurred at an interesting artistic moment for Browne. On his early recordings, Browne tended to "abandon" his own playing in his arrangements in favor of what his band came up with. But when he began alternating band and solo shows, he grew to "want to keep what I do, what I enjoy and like about my playing."

Lindley's presence has had another effect, too. "The band really enjoys David so much," he says. "You find them all standing around the stage watching his set because he's so full of surprises." This is a guy whose set includes a Blind Willie McTell tune played on bouzouki and a Steve Earl tune played on oud. After following the tour, I can attest that the man never even flirts with playing a tune or solo the same way twice. A new performance by David Lindley is, indeed, a new performance.

Lindley himself is no slouch in the guitar knowledge department. "He was the guy I first met who had all these instruments salted away," observes Browne. He recalls asking Lindley about instruments he'd not seen for a while and "he could haul it out. He was a real instrument hoarder, and I got that from him." Perhaps most importantly, "David would get out these different guitars and play them entirely differently. The guitars really wanted a different style."

As Browne puts it, it's "the search for the optimum sound." ♬

Stay

Jackson Browne on Songwriting

INTRODUCTION BY JASON VERLINDE

PHOTOGRAPHY BY DOUG VAN DOREN AND LIZ DANAHEY

WHEN JACKSON BROWNE WAS A CHILD, his family (living overseas in Germany) transplanted to Southern California. No, not to your typical tract housing or a bungalow by the beach, but to the mission-inspired Abbey San Encino that his grandfather (and namesake, Clyde Browne) built by hand to house a legendary letterpress print shop, the Abbey Press. All told, it's a fitting typecast (yes, pun intended) for one of the more literary-minded songsmiths of our time.

Five decades later, Browne walked photographers Doug Van Doren, Liz Danahey and I through his other famous home, his recording studio in Santa Monica. Here, in his own words, Browne reveals his songwriting process, how his tunes have evolved over the years, some of his favorite guitar tales and much more.

— Jason Verlinde

If every guitar has a song inside of it, Browne isn't going to be running out of tunes anytime soon. Here, various incarnations of his Gibson Jackson Browne signature model guitar sit alongside his vintage acoustics and electrics. Behind his right elbow in the blue suede is one of the earliest Dumble amplifiers.

A Mysterious Process

[Songwriting] happens a number of different ways, sometimes it's just a phrase that gets stuck in my head that embodies an idea.

It's a pretty mysterious process and I wish I had some sort of formula, because I would do it more. But it's really a way of weaving something out of an initial thought.

The hardest thing is when you get a piece of music and the music gets developed without any words and then you have to put words to it. That's hard! The other way is the best. I like to write with a MiniDisc so that if I'm playing and something happens, I can usually get a bit of it.

The song is a process of me cross-examining myself. Once you've said one or two things, then it's like, well, what about it? It's been a long time since stuff just came out or flowed out in one night. Normally now, it happens over a longer period of time.

My first way of writing was to be alone late at night, when everything else was done. When I was in high school and at home, that was when it was quiet. I could be away from where people were sleeping and be in the kitchen by myself. I'd stay up and write.

Sometimes I've written stuff based on soundcheck jams. I've always recorded soundchecks anyway in case something like this happens. "Barricades of Heaven" and the song "Never Stop" came out of soundchecks.

I think for me the real writing happens once the song gets going. There's a series of opportunities to really ask myself what I'm really trying to say.

Writing Tools

I write [songs] on whatever I've got around. Sometimes in the hotel room, I've got a guitar that I'm traveling with. It goes on and off the bus.

I record everything that I'm working on to a little MiniDisc so that I have an example of that kind of playing. A lot of times [listening back], it's really surprising — what was *that* guitar? It made me play like that? You finally realize, "Oh, it was that time I had the guitar that I normally have in E-flat tuning, but I was in the hotel and I wound up putting that in standard."

But that's not so important, because by the time something becomes a song, it's been tried on a lot of different instruments.

Gathering Meaning

There are songs that I still do that I wrote when I was 16 or 18 and it's never a nostalgia thing. It's only that the song has continued to gather meaning, the memories that have attached themself to that song in the intervening years. It's not that I'm nostalgic for that time. And even when it was inspired by a particular thing, I'm rarely thinking about the person I wrote the song for at the time. I'm thinking more about the situation. If a song is written well, it's really about anyone's life anyway. By the time a song is written, I'm not really attached to what inspired it as I am attached to the song and the emotional truth of that experience.

Browne's Gibson SG features a Teisco pickup in the neck position. "David Lindley gave the pickup to me on my 50th birthday," Browne remembers. "He said, 'Here, grasshopper, try this.'" Since the Teisco foil pickup was reflective and stood out on the SG's black pickguard, Browne has since given it a black baked enamel finish. "I got from Lindley the bug of seeing what you can do to a guitar, experimenting," Browne says. "Some people don't do it, they just collect classic guitars. Lindley has always been someone to throw a different neck on a guitar or play with the pickups... that's how he came upon some of the great tones."

There's something that happens in the songwriting process that is like a filter: the experiences and the details become universal because the people listening to them make them that. You're seeing what's going on in the song and you're seeing the only thing you could possibly see... pictures from your own life. That becomes yours.

If you hear "Wild Horses," you don't think about Mick Jagger and Marianne Faithful. You think about whoever you were hanging around with at the time. It's not about them; it's about you.

The Revisionist

There's probably nothing I've written that I couldn't touch up and make better now. I wrote "These Days" when I was 16 and I changed a few of the lyrics when I was 22 or 23. Some people sing the original lyrics, and they're good; it's just very different than the way I feel. The original lyric of "These Days" has this line "I'll stop my dreaming" and I didn't think that was quite true for me. I changed it to "I'll keep on

Browne was one of amp guru Alexander "Howard" Dumble's earliest customers. He still owns a few Dumble amplifiers, including this Overdrive Special. He has, however, parted ways with one of the more famous Dumbles. In the '90s, he sold the Dumble bass amp that Stevie Ray Vaughan used on *Texas Flood* (which was recorded at Browne's old studio in downtown Los Angeles). "For a while we had an all-Dumble stage. Every cabinet was Dumble!" Browne says with a smile.

moving." I wanted a song that was that sort of down to have some hope in it.

I wrote that song when I was 16 and I think Gregg Allman learned it a couple of years later. He recorded it on his *Laid Back* album. And when I heard it, I fucking loved it. I rediscovered the song. But in order for me to sing it at that time — I was in my early 20s — I had to revise it.

The song "The Birds of St. Marks" was made by a guitar tune I wrote. Imagine the Byrds playing with a rock beat but with this chimey guitar... I could never pull it off! I wrote that when I was 18 and I didn't even think about it again until I was talking with a friend and I wanted to show them the song, but I was sitting at the piano.

I just started playing it on the piano and this whole sort of page turned and suddenly there was this completely new way of playing it; it just threw the guitar idea out the window. The song was suddenly a whole, finished song that I could play. That's the beauty of any kind of writing on an instrument. You can switch to another instrument and get another perspective... or a different guitar, which is why I have this ridiculous number of guitars on stage.

"For Everyman" came to me, but then I spent six months writing the back half of the song. The first verse comes along and you think that's it! But then what? Some songs are really hard to write because they're so simple. There's almost nothing left to say. And then that's the job of somehow making the all too necessary second verse say something evocative.

Browne is not known for his Telecaster playing, but this 1954 Blackguard has a good lost and found tale behind it. "Somewhere around my second album, I bought it from a guy who was hanging around Los Angeles. I think I paid 500 bucks for it," Browne remembers. "Guys in my various bands have used it -- it got played a lot by Danny Kortchmar and Waddy Wachtel. It has such an amazing tone."

To pay for some studio upgrades, Browne eventually put it on consignment at a guitar store, where it was purchased by the Hard Rock Cafe. "I wasn't playing it; I'm not sentimental about these things," he says. "At one point, I was in a Hard Rock Cafe Hotel and I was looking through their catalog of their guitar collection and I didn't see my guitar. Everybody in the world was in this book: the greats, the *near* greats and the definitely *not* greats!"

Concerned about where it ended up, Browne had a friend reach out to the Hard Rock organization. The Tele was located at an outdoor bar in Hawaii, hanging behind some Plexiglass. Browne bought it back. It tanned from all the sun exposure and received a few holes from its wall mount but, Browne says, "it's still an amazing guitar; a great one."

Recording room at Groove Masters, the guitar playground and recording studio that Jackson Browne owns in Santa Monica, California.

Browne keeps this Fender Newporter tuned a half-step low and uses it primarily on his tune "Off of Wonderland." The guitar now has a Trance Audio Amulet in it. "If you play it acoustically, it's kind of bright and not very deep," Browne says. "It's very even."

Filtration Process

We're used to recording everything. To me, that's the only way to get the very best of what happened during a tour, make sure everything got recorded. Every now and then something doesn't get recorded, it's pretty upsetting to think that something got away, because you come in and you pick your six or seven best versions of a song, and then you choose between them and decide which one. It's really a filtration process. And then it sounds like it was done in one night.

I'm trying to make it as ideal a listening encounter as possible. You're hearing the most amazing things that got played in the course of a tour, but it sounds like it really came down in one evening.

The truth is that, in the case of "Running on Empty," that version of that song was the only time that got played that way out of 30 dates.

Songs That Won't Fit

One time, I left a hit song off the album because it wasn't part of the thing I was trying to say in the album… "Somebody's Baby." I gave them the song for the movie [*Fast Times at Ridgemont High*], because I wasn't going to put it on the record [*Hold Out*], even after it was a hit…

Cameron [Crowe] said, "Do you have any songs for this soundtrack?"

I said, "Well, we've got *this* song."

I wasn't thinking to keep the most commercial songs or keep the best. I just didn't think like that, even later.

So, the movie came out and the song was the hit from the movie.

Somebody asked, "You're going to put that on the record, right?" I'm going, "No. It doesn't fit." They weren't going to argue with me, but it was my cue to pay attention. I've always been a little bit thick that way; I don't really always get it.

150 Takes

I literally have 150 reels of the same song, "Tender Is the Night," and that was pre-drum machine! And for every one of those takes I had a full band in the studio downtown. We must have played that song for a month.

It's still a joke amongst our friends. This friend of mine heard some people talking in a sushi bar. "Yeah, I heard them playing this song… and I came in there, like two weeks later, and they were recording the same song!" He leaned in a little further and realized that they were talking about me!

> ▶ To see an exclusive video of Browne performing "Something Fine" on his vintage Gibson Roy Smeck, visit us online at fretboardjournal.com/video.

Browne needs to be able to amplify nearly every guitar in his collection. A 1940s Gibson LG-2 sports a Teisco pickup. "The Teisco pickup is a flat, single-coil pickup and has a really warm response," Browne says.

Gibson Roy Smeck Guitars

Modifying vintage guitars is usually discouraged, but not here

I N 1934, GIBSON BEGAN PRODUCING two Roy Smeck signature models. Both were modeled after Gibson's new slope shoulder dreadnought "Jumbo" body style, though with 12 frets clear of the body instead of 14, a deeper body with no noticeable taper in depth from neckblock to endblock (averaging about 4.25 inches), a "Hawaiian" setup with raised nut and flush ivoroid fingerboard markers instead of frets and a non-compensated saddle set at a right angle to the strings. The Radio Grande had rosewood back and sides, with those built before mid-1935 sporting Brazilian rosewood while the later guitars are made of Indian rosewood. The Stage Deluxe, meanwhile, featured mahogany back and sides.

Many of the original Smecks have been converted for use in "Spanish-style" of play, which usually necessitates installation of frets, lowering the nut, a neck reset to provide for a proper neck angle and re-slotting the bridge to accommodate an angled saddle. Some players also choose to have the very wide neck — ranging between 2.25 and 2 inches at the nut — narrowed to make playing them a bit more comfortable. The Indian rosewood reissues come from the factory as "conversions," sporting all of the typical modifications and a 1-13/16 inch nut width. Browne's new signature model guitar from Gibson features one interesting twist on the above: the singer-songwriter selected sustainably-farmed walnut for the back and sides.

— John Thomas

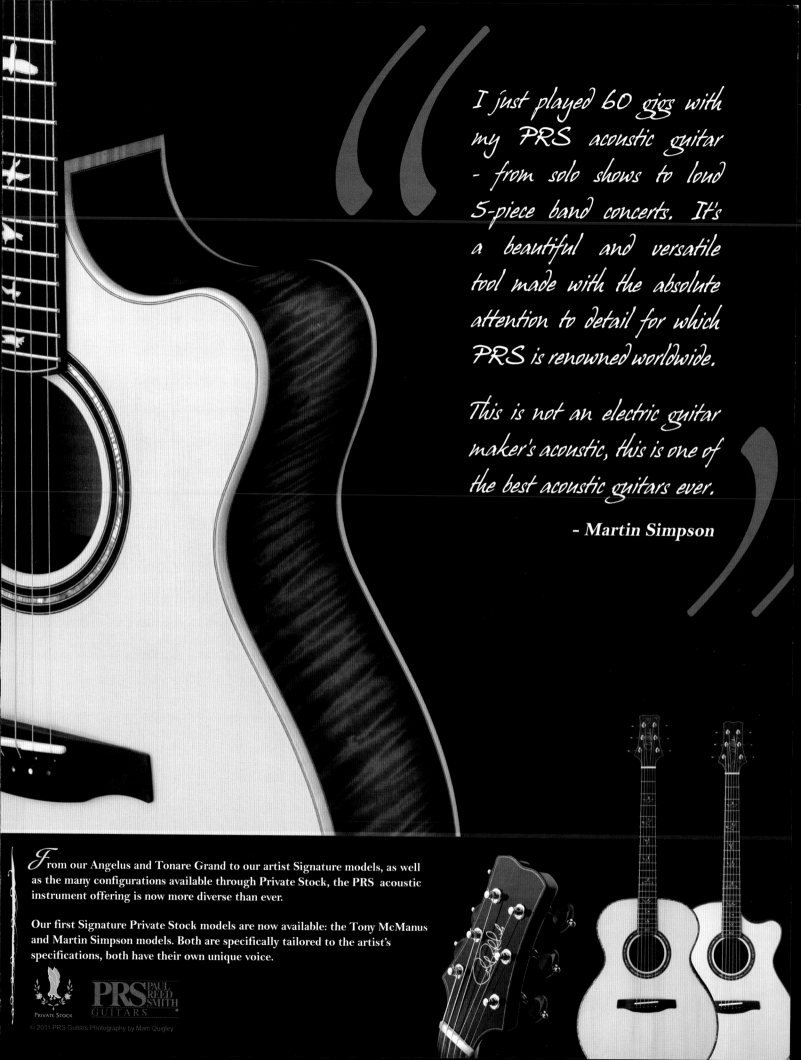

I just played 60 gigs with my PRS acoustic guitar - from solo shows to loud 5-piece band concerts. It's a beautiful and versatile tool made with the absolute attention to detail for which PRS is renowned worldwide.

This is not an electric guitar maker's acoustic, this is one of the best acoustic guitars ever.

- Martin Simpson

From our Angelus and Tonare Grand to our artist Signature models, as well as the many configurations available through Private Stock, the PRS acoustic instrument offering is now more diverse than ever.

Our first Signature Private Stock models are now available: the Tony McManus and Martin Simpson models. Both are specifically tailored to the artist's specifications, both have their own unique voice.

PRIVATE STOCK

PRS PAUL REED SMITH GUITARS

Left: Vintage photo of Hutchins' grandfather, Lloyd Hutchins, the Martin's original owner.
Right: The original '37 Martin on the left and Arnold's interpretation on the right.

All in the Family

A 1937 Martin mimicked by John Arnold

STEVEN HUTCHINS IS A LUCKY GUITARIST. He not only takes care of his grandfather's 1937 shadetop Martin 00-18, he was able to convince acclaimed guitar builder and historian John Arnold to build a replica of it.

Newport, Tennessee's Arnold may not be a household name, but he's one of the world's foremost experts on tonewoods and an acclaimed repairperson. Along with the late Ted Davis, Arnold helped bring about a renaissance of red spruce in acoustic guitars. And, though he's sold the spruce that he's foraged around the Smoky Mountains to some of the world's best-known builders, he's only made around 70 of his own guitars. As a comparison, fellow builder Wayne Henderson has built over 500 guitars.

It should be noted that there's a Henderson connection here, too. "Wayne Henderson set the neck on the Martin in June of 2007," Hutchins remembers. "That was the first repair that had ever been on that guitar." These days, Hutchins plays the Arnold more than the original Martin, though having spent a few minutes with each, we can attest to both being very special guitars.

— Jason Verlinde

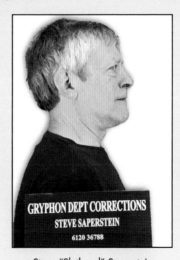

FINE HANDMADE ACOUSTIC GUITARS
& STRINGED MUSICAL INSTRUMENTS
OCTOBER 22 & 23, 2011
BEARSVILLE THEATER
WOODSTOCK, NEW YORK
WWW.WOODSTOCKINVITATIONAL.COM

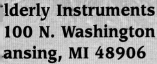

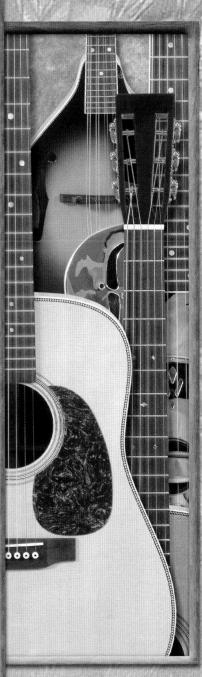

celebrating our fifteenth anniversary...

HUSS & DALTON
MUSICAL INSTRUMENTS
Staunton | Virginia | USA

hussanddalton.com

Jack Looney Photography

Case Closed

FOR THE MOST PART, instrument cases are like pirate's treasure chests: they contain wonderful things but they are not wonderful on their own. But every now and then a case shows up that is as exciting as the instrument it protects. Take this old canvas ukulele case, for example.

It's perhaps one of the cheapest cases ever made, but at some time in the 1920s, its owner decided to decorate it with hand-drawn images. The uke turned up at a now-closed Fresno shop called Archer's Music, where it was snagged by the store's repair tech, Mike Newton. He doesn't recall anything about the woman who brought it in, but he knew immediately that the case was as cool as the Mossman uke it contained.

The first thing that caught Newton's eye was the large drawing of a woman wearing a brimless cloche hat, a style that was pretty much the uniform of a 1920's flapper. The byline below the portrait reads "Honolulu, T.H.," which meant that the artist decorated the case when the islands were still known as the Territory of Hawaii.

On one side of the case, the artist (who signed the case R. Miyahara) drew what looks like a landscape of Waikiki with Diamond Head in the background. You can see the outrigger canoes on the shore and a large structure that resembles the Royal Hawaiian Hotel, which opened in 1927. Was Miyahara a tourist from Japan or did he or she live in Honolulu?

The most personal bit of decoration is also the most mysterious. The meaning of the arrow through the two hearts is clear enough, but what about the black underneath them? Is it an emphatic underline or did R. carefully ink out the name of his or her paramour? And what about the question mark? Does it signify that R. knows the name of the next significant other and doesn't want to tell or does it mean that R. doesn't know who he or she will fall in love with next? Whatever the meaning, I hope it turned out well for R.

As for the uke in the case? It was made by George Mossman, who built ukes in Hawaii during the 1920s. His instruments are fairly scarce these days, but in his time he was quite well known. A 1928 *Time* magazine said Mossman's instruments "have earned him the title of 'Hawaiian Strad.'"

— **Tom Walzem**

A 1920 ukulele case with a story

These inexpensive canvas cases are now known as "bottom dumpers" because, over time, the leather "hinge" that attaches the lid to the shell of the case rots away, making it easy for the instrument to fall out.

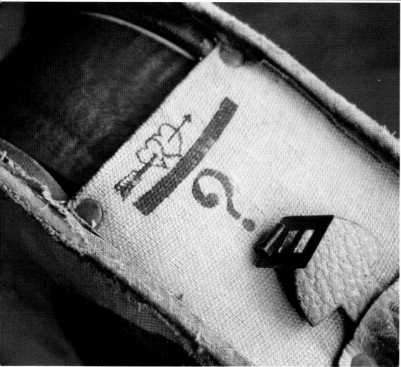

Along with building fine ukuleles, George Mossman was a champion of Hawaiian culture. In 1929 he started a Hawaiian language school, this at a time when it was forbidden to speak Hawaiian or dance the hula in the public schools. In 1932, he opened a replica Hawaiian village where he gave lessons in hula dancing (40 lessons for $10), ukulele lessons and Hawaiian language lessons.

Guy Charles and his daughter Adrienne at Alsia Farm
Cornwall, UK

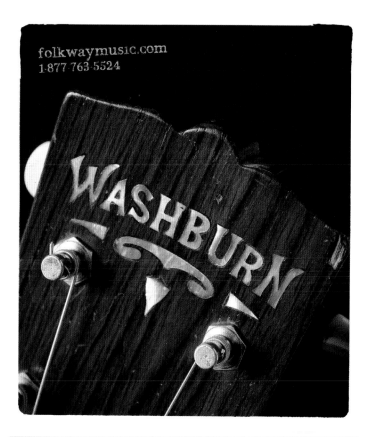
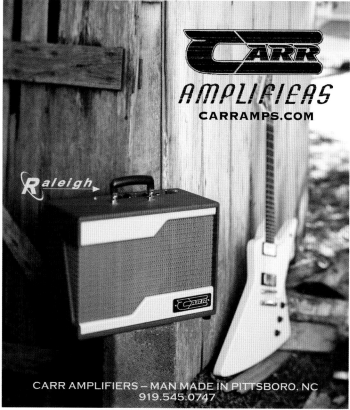

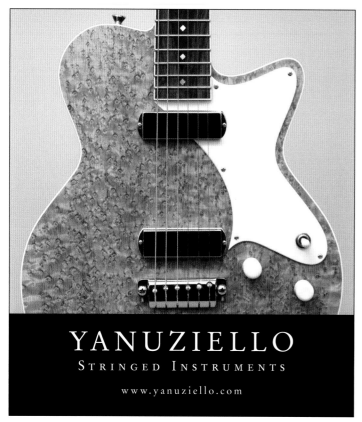

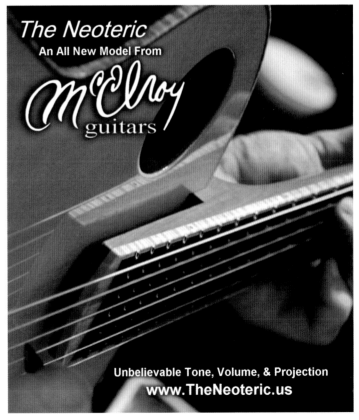

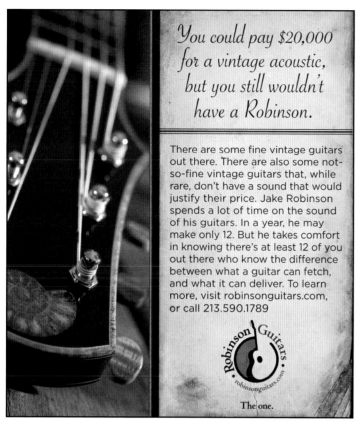

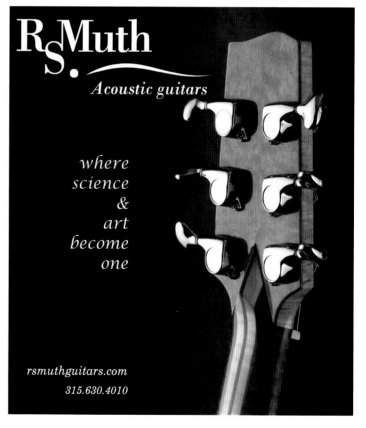

CONTRIBUTORS

RACHEL BLECKMAN'S interest in photography and music began at an early age. In 1989 she embarked on a six-year project documenting Deadheads following The Grateful Dead. Since then, Rachel has been covering the music scene in the San Francisco Bay area. Along with her photographs in *The Fretboard Journal* her work has been published in *Rolling Stone*, *Guitar Player* and *Blender*.

LYNN DONALDSON'S images appear regularly in magazines such as *Travel + Leisure*, *Sunset*, *Via* and the *New York Times*. Based in Livingston, Montana, she recently started blogging about food and travel in Montana's High Plains for the Montana Office of Tourism.

RICH KIENZLE is one of the premier music journalists working in the field today. He's the author of *Southwest Shuffle: Pioneers of Honky-Tonk, Western Swing and Country Jazz* and *Great Guitarists: The Most Influential Players in Jazz, Blues, Country and Rock* as well as the liner notes for numerous Bear Family box sets.

A native of Raleigh, North Carolina, **JOHN PEDEN** moved to San Francisco in the '60s with the Heavenly Blues Band. When the band members went their separate ways, John put down his guitar, picked up a Leica and set out on a photographic career that has spanned four decades. His work is featured in the books *The Soul of Tone, The Stratocaster Chronicles* and *Fender: The Sound Heard 'Round the World*. In 2011 he has started a new venture, "Peden's Vintage" located in his wife, Paulette's, antique store in New Preston, Connecticut, specializing in the restoration and sale of classic guitar amplifiers.

THOMAS PETILLO is a nationally renowned fine-art and commercial photographer based in Nashville, Tennessee. His most recent project, *Just A Way Out*, is currently touring museums in the United States.

JOHN THOMAS is a law professor, freelance writer, film producer and a fingerpicking guitarist. He's also a founding member and president of the Board of Directors of the Buddy Holly Guitar Foundation.

DOUG VAN DOREN has been a contributing photographer to *The Fretboard Journal* since its inaugural issue. He has photographed a number of artists over the years including Tom Brousseau, David Lindley, Ben Harper and Wilco. He lives in Los Angeles with his wife and son.

ANDY VOLK is a 20-year veteran of the Boston media community and is trained in art, film and music. He has worked as a video writer, producer and director as well as graphic designer. A musician since his teens, Andy plays guitar, mandolin and steel guitar. He is the author of *Slide Rules: Tunings for Lap Steel, Bottleneck, Resophonic*, and *Indian Slide Guitar For 6, 8, 10-string Guitars* and *Lap Steel Guitar*.

JOE YANUZIELLO is a Toronto-based luthier. His musical tastes run the gamut, which is evidenced by the wide variety of acoustic and electric stringed instruments he produces. His appreciation of the history and development of classic instruments informs his building style, and defines his distinctive design choices.

STATEMENT OF OWNERSHIP, MANAGEMENT AND CIRCULATION PS Form 3526. March 21, 2011. *The Fretboard Journal*, Publication No. 1558-0326 is published four times a year in February, May, August and November. Annual subscription price is $40.00. The complete mailing address of the Office of Publication is 2221 NW 56th St. Suite 101, Seattle, WA 98107. The full and complete name of the publisher is Jason Verlinde at the above address. The editor is Michael John Simmons at 2221 NW 56th St. Suite 101, Seattle, WA 98107. There are no known bond holders, mortgages or other security holder, owing or holding 1% or more of total amount of bonds, mortgages or other securities. The owners of Occasional Publishing, Inc., Jason Verlinde of Seattle, WA and Michael Simmons of Mountain View, CA. The extent and nature of circulation is as follows: A. Total average number copies each issue during preceding 12 months (net press run) is 21,766; actual number of single issue published nearing to filing date is 20,530. B. Paid and/or requested circulation, 1. Total average number copies each issue during preceding 12 months of mail subscriptions (paid and/or requested) is 4,977; actual number of single issue subscriptions nearest to filing date is 4,769. 3. Total average number copies each issue during preceding 12 months of sales through dealers and carriers, street vendors and counter sales is 6,172; actual number copies sold through dealers and carriers, street vendors and counter sales is 5,223. C. (Sum of B1, B2, B3, B4) Average number copies of each issue during preceding 12 months of total paid and/or requested circulation is 11,190; actual number copies of single issue published nearest filing to date is 10,036. D-E. Average number copies each issue during preceding 12 months for free distribution by mail, carrier or other means (samples, complimentary and other free copies) is 122; actual number copies of single issue published nearest to filing date is 122. F. Total distribution of sum C and E for average number copies each issue during preceding 12 months is 11,312; actual number copies of single issue published nearest to filing date is 10,158. G. Average number copies each issue during preceding 12 months of copies not distributed for 1. Office use, leftover, unaccounted, spoiled after printing is 10,454; actual number of copies of single issue published nearest to filing date is 10,372. H. Total (sum 15G and H should equal net press run shown in A) average number copies each issue during preceding 12 months is 21,766; actual number copies of single issue published nearest to filing date is 20,530. I. Paid and/or Requested Circulation equals 99% of total actual copies (average during preceding 12 months) and 99% (single issue published nearest to filing date). I certify that the statements made by me above are correct and complete. Jason Verlinde, Publisher.

Featured Products

Collings MF5-O
Blond Finish

Kamaka HF-1
Soprano Ukulele

Santa Cruz
Baritone

Collings CW
Adi / Rosewood

Bourgeois OM
All-Mahogany

Huss & Dalton
Mini Jumbo

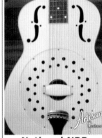
National NRP
Collegian

Collings I-35 LC
Laminate Body

Welcome to **Artisan Guitars**... _not_ your average guitar shop.

The very concept of a guitar shop in Nashville is hardly unique. However, when you visit the legendary Music City, as you might expect, there is a lot of history & heritage to live up to. With some of the world's finest songwriters, session players, and famous recording studios; it beckons visions of Guitar Mecca for players from around the world.

Living up to those high expectations, Artisan Guitars proudly represents some of the world's finest acoustic guitar builders of this century, luthiers who in their own right are artists in every sense of the term. They provide the future heirloom quality instruments that our children and grandchildren will inherit as their musical heritage, today.

Gift Certificates now available!

New from Bourgeois view all

New from Collings view all

Like   479 people like this.

Search for:

[Search]

Instruments

Arriving Soon
Acoustic Guitars
   Bourgeois Guitars
   Collings Acoustics
   Composite Acoustics
   Huss & Dalton
   National Reso-Phonic
   Santa Cruz
   Other Acoustics
Banjos
Bass Guitars
Dobros
Electric Guitars
   Collings Electrics
   National Electrics
   Other Electrics
Mandolin Family
   A-Style
   F-Style
Ukuleles
   Collings Ukuleles
   Kamaka Ukuleles
   National Ukuleles
Violin Family
Vintage Instruments
Pre-Owned
Recently Adopted

Amplification

Bose PA Systems
Guitar Amplifiers
   Carr Amps
   Fishman Amps
   Trace Acoustics
   Ultrasound Amps
   Other Amps
Microphones
Pickups
Preamps

Accessories

Artisan Merchandise
   Hats
   Gift Certificates
   Shirts
   Tickets
   Books

Toll Free 866-265-5993
Local 615-595-2544
info@artisanguitars.com

Shop Hours: 10am - 5pm
Monday - Saturday

Layaway Available!

We Ship Internationally!

Upcoming Events

view entire schedule

Featured Item

Fretboard Journal Issue 19 – Fall 2010 – Featuring Tim O'Brien and Sam Bush

Fretboard JOURNAL

News and Media

Audio Samples
Newsletter Archive
Shop News
Testimonials
Videos

Subscribe to Newsletter

Email:

[Submit]

Newest Instruments

TAILPIECE

PHOTO BY MARK JOHNSTON

PLENTY OF ACOUSTIC GUITAR BUILDERS WILL PROMISE TO BUILD YOU A "CANNON," BUT LARRY POGREBA MAY BE THE ONLY ONE WHO CAN FULFILL THAT ORDER.

FROM SOMEWHERE DEEP IN MONTANA, WITNESS DOUG PICKERING WRITES, "IF YOU LOOK IN THE SMOKE YOU CAN SEE THE SMALL TUPPERWARE BOWL THAT HELD THE GUNPOWDER. ABOVE THAT, THE LARGER BLACK OBJECT IS BURNT PAPER PLATES USED FOR WADDING. FURTHER UP IS A SMALL BLACK OBJECT, WHICH IS THE BOWLING BALL."

WE'RE TOLD THE BALL FROM POGREBA'S CANNON WILL ULTIMATELY LAND ACROSS THE PASTURE ON THE FAR RIDGE... PAST THE PLOWED FIELD YOU SEE.

IN GUITARS AND IN LIFE, IT'S ALL ABOUT PROJECTION...

— JV